MathFlare

Name: _____________________

Class: __________

Teacher: _____________________

Introduction

As parents and educators, we recognize the pivotal role mathematics plays in shaping a child's academic journey and future success. Yet, the path to mathematical proficiency can often seem daunting, fraught with challenges and complexities. That's where the transformative power of MathFlare Workbooks shine through, illuminating the way forward with clarity, precision, and purpose.

Introducing MathFlare Workbooks – a beacon of guidance, a testament to excellence, and a catalyst for achievement. Crafted with meticulous care and expertise, MathFlare Workbooks stand as paragons of educational excellence, designed to nurture young minds, ignite a passion for learning, and develop a deep-rooted understanding of mathematical concepts.

Picture this: your child eagerly delves into the pages of Mathflare Workbook, greeted by a step-by-step guide illuminated with vivid examples that demystify complex mathematical concepts. With each turn of the page, they embark on a journey of discovery, encountering thoughtfully curated practice questions that reinforce learning and hone problem-solving skills. And when they unveil the answers to those very questions, a sense of accomplishment blossoms within them – a tangible reward for their hard work and dedication.

But MathFlare Workbooks are more than just tools for learning; they are pathways to comprehension, fostering a deep-seated understanding of mathematical concepts through a sequential, logical flow. From fundamental principles to advanced problem-solving strategies, every chapter builds upon the last, ensuring a robust foundation upon which future knowledge can be constructed.

As parents, we yearn for nothing more than to see our children thrive, to witness the spark of inspiration ignited within them as they conquer academic challenges with confidence and poise. MathFlare Workbooks serve as partners in this noble endeavor, offering not just practice questions, but the keys to unlocking a world of opportunity.

And for teachers, MathFlare Workbooks stand as invaluable allies in the quest to cultivate mathematical proficiency in the classroom. With answers readily available, instructors can focus on guiding and nurturing their students, confident in the knowledge that MathFlare Workbooks provide a solid framework upon which to build.

In the pages of MathFlare Workbooks, we find not just the promise of academic excellence, but the seeds of a brighter tomorrow. So let us embrace the power of mathematics, let us champion the journey of learning, and let us pave the way for a generation of young minds poised to shape the world. With MathFlare Workbooks as our guide, the possibilities are infinite, and the future, bright.

Table of Contents

MathFlare
Grade 2
MATH WORKBOOK
Step by Step Guide and Essential Practice with Answers
Addition Subtraction
Multiplication
Place Value and Expanded Notations
Geometry
MathFlare Publishing

MathFlare
Grade 2-3
MATH WORKBOOK
Step by Step Guide and Essential Practice with Answers
Addition Subtraction
Multiplication and Division
Place Value and Expanded Notations
Geometry
MathFlare Publishing

MathFlare
Grade 3
MATH WORKBOOK
Step by Step Guide and Essential Practice with Answers
Multiplication and Division
Decimals
Place Value and Expanded Notations
Fractions and Geometry
MathFlare Publishing

MathFlare
Grade 1
MATH WORKBOOK
Step by Step Guide and Essential Practice with Answers
Counting and Numbers
Addition and Subtraction
Place Value and Expanded Notations
Understanding Time
MathFlare Publishing

MathFlare
Grade 1-2
MATH WORKBOOK
Step by Step Guide and Essential Practice with Answers
Counting and Numbers
Addition and Subtraction
Place Value and Expanded Notations
Understanding Time
MathFlare Publishing

MathFlare
Grade 3-4
MATH WORKBOOK
Step by Step Guide and Essential Practice with Answers
Addition Subtraction
Multiplication Division
Place Value and Expanded Notations
Fractions and Geometry
MathFlare Publishing

MathFlare
Grade 4
MATH WORKBOOK
Step by Step Guide and Essential Practice with Answers
Addition Subtraction
Multiplication Division
Place Value and Expanded Notations
Fractions and Geometry
MathFlare Publishing

MathFlare
Grade 4-5
MATH WORKBOOK
Step by Step Guide and Essential Practice with Answers
Multiplication Division
Place Value and Expanded Notations
Fractions and Geometry
Unit Conversion
MathFlare Publishing

MathFlare
MATH
WORKBOOK
5
Step by Step Guide
and Essential Practice
with Answers
Multiplication
Division
Place Value and
Expanded
Notations
Fractions
and Geometry
Unit
Conversion
MathFlare Publishing

MathFlare
MATH
WORKBOOK
5-6
Step by Step Guide
and Essential Practice
with Answers
Multiplication
Division
Place Value and
Expanded
Notations
Fractions
and Geometry
Units and
Statistics
MathFlare Publishing

MathFlare
MATH
WORKBOOK
6
Step by Step Guide
and Essential Practice
with Answers
Integers and
Statistics
Arithmetic and
Pre-Algebra
Fractions
and Geometry
Ratio and
Percentage
MathFlare Publishing

MathFlare
MATH
WORKBOOK
6-7
Step by Step Guide
and Essential Practice
with Answers
Arithmetic and
Pre-Algebra
Ratio, Percent
Proportion
Geometry
Statistics
MathFlare Publishing

MathFlare
MATH
WORKBOOK
7
Step by Step Guide
and Essential Practice
with Answers
Pre-Algebra
Ratio, Percent
Proportion
Geometry
Statistics
MathFlare Publishing

MathFlare
MATH
WORKBOOK
7-8
Step by Step Guide
and Essential Practice
with Answers
Pre-Algebra
Ratio, Percent
Proportion
Geometry and
Cartesian
Plane
Statistics
MathFlare Publishing

MathFlare
MATH
WORKBOOK
8-9
Step by Step Guide
and Essential Practice
with Answers
Pre-Algebra
Ratio, Proportion
and Percentage
Linear
Equations
Geometry and
Cartesian Plane
MathFlare Publishing

MathFlare
MATH
WORKBOOK
8
Step by Step Guide
and Essential Practice
with Answers
Pre-Algebra
Percentage
Linear
Equations
Geometry
MathFlare Publishing

Multiplication and Division

Multiplication

Multiplication is an easy way of adding numbers together quickly. Instead of adding the same number repeatedly, we use multiplication to find the total much faster.

For instance, rather than adding 2 + 2 + 2 + 2 + 2, we can multiply 2 by 5 to get the same result: 2 x 5 = 10.

Here, the first number (2) is called the multiplicand, second number (5) is the multiplier. The answer we get, in this case, 10, is called the product.

Let's think of multiplication as repeated addition.

Take 2 x 5, for example. It means adding 2 together five times, which we can illustrate as: 2 + 2 + 2 + 2 + 2 = 10

Multiplication can also be visualized as groups of objects. Imagine we have 2 groups, each containing 5 oranges.

To find the total number of oranges, we multiply the number of groups (2) by the number of oranges in each group (5):

2 groups of 5 oranges = 10 oranges

Expressed as multiplication: 2 x 5 = 10

In summary, multiplication offers various ways to approach it: through repeated addition or by envisioning groups of objects. It's a powerful tool that makes solving math problems much quicker and more efficient!

We can also use the following table to quickly remember multiplication facts. The intersection of two points shows the product of two numbers.

For instance, the product of 5 x 6 = 30, or 6 x 5 = 30.

	1	2	3	4	5	6	7	8	9	10
1	1	2	3	4	5	6	7	8	9	10
2	2	4	6	8	10	12	14	16	18	20
3	3	6	9	12	15	18	21	24	27	30
4	4	8	12	16	20	24	28	32	36	40
5	5	10	15	20	25	30	35	40	45	50
6	6	12	18	24	30	36	42	48	54	60
7	7	14	21	28	35	42	49	56	63	70
8	8	16	24	32	40	48	56	64	72	80
9	9	18	27	36	45	54	63	72	81	90
10	10	20	30	40	50	60	70	80	90	100

Long Division and Remainders

Division is like the opposite of multiplication. It's all about sharing or distributing items equally among a certain number of groups or people.

When we divide one number by another, we're essentially splitting a number into equal parts. We're figuring out how many groups of a certain size can be made from that number.

For instance, let's divide 20 by 4.

When we divide 20 by 4, we're essentially asking, "How many groups of size 4 can we make from 20?"

Now, there are several parts or terms involved in the division process:

- **Dividend:** This is the number being divided, which in this case, is 20.

- **Divisor:** This is the number we're dividing by, which is 4.

- **Quotient:** This is the answer we get after dividing. It tells us how many groups of divisors can be made from the dividend. In this case, the answer is 5.

- **Remainder:** when the divisor doesn't evenly divide the dividend, we get the remainder.

So, when we divide 20 by 4, we found out that 5 groups of 4 can be made from 20.

Let's solve problems from exercises:

```
            08,464.6
      10 ) 84,646
           - 0
            84
           - 80
             46
           - 40
             64
           - 60
             46
           - 40
             60
           - 60
              0
```

```
      8,965 R1
   9 ) 80,686
     - 72
       86
     - 81
       58
     - 54
       46
     - 45
        1
```

Multi Digit Multiplication

```
          70,278
      ×    2,965
   +    351390
   +   421668
   +  632502
   + 140556
   = 208374270
```

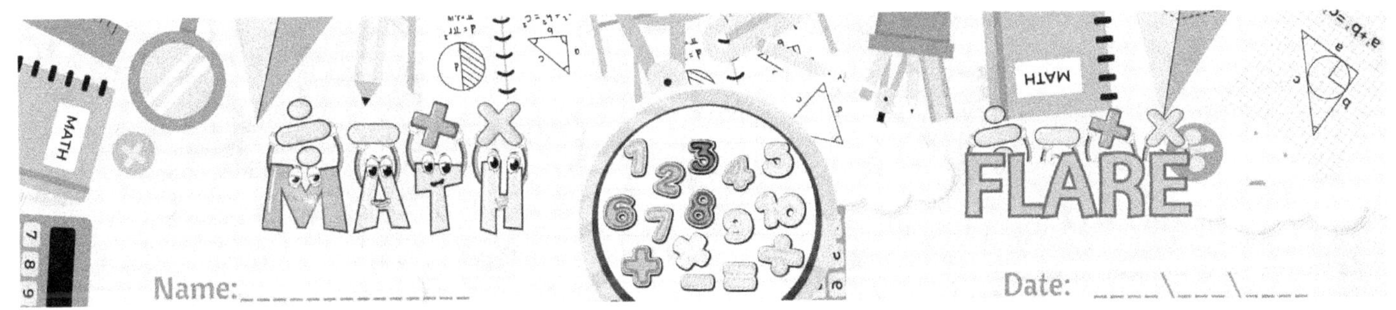

Name:________________   Date: ______________

Multi Digit Multiplication

Find the product.

1. 83,097
  × 4,790

2. 31,326
  × 1,091

3. 71,478
  × 9,681

4. 40,333
  × 9,724

5. 38,242
  × 4,351

6. 14,412
  × 3,965

7. 47,498
  × 6,324

8. 94,352
  × 5,101

9. 14,786
  × 7,878

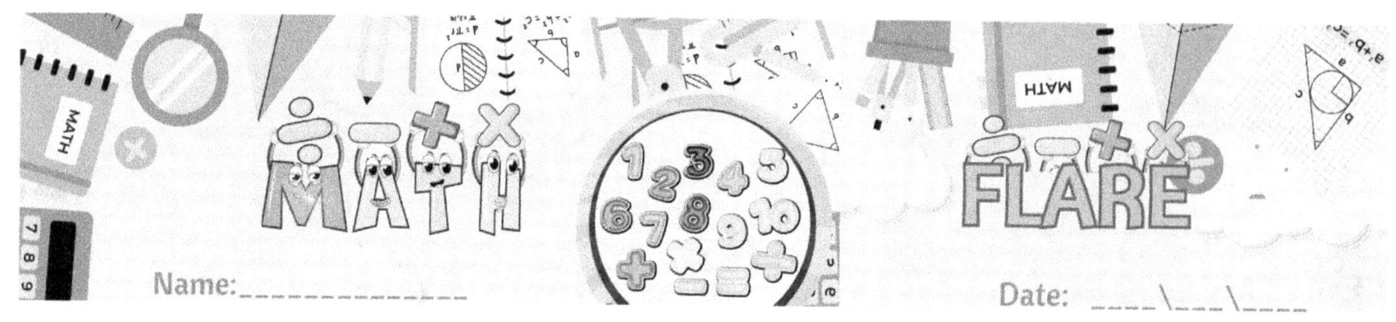

10.   34,180
  ×   2,984

11.   27,828
  ×   6,040

12.   10,366
  ×   7,881

13.   36,028
  ×   1,285

14.   20,560
  ×   9,398

15.   90,779
  ×   3,867

16.   63,037
  ×   2,840

17.   50,563
  ×   7,360

18.   54,373
  ×   6,588

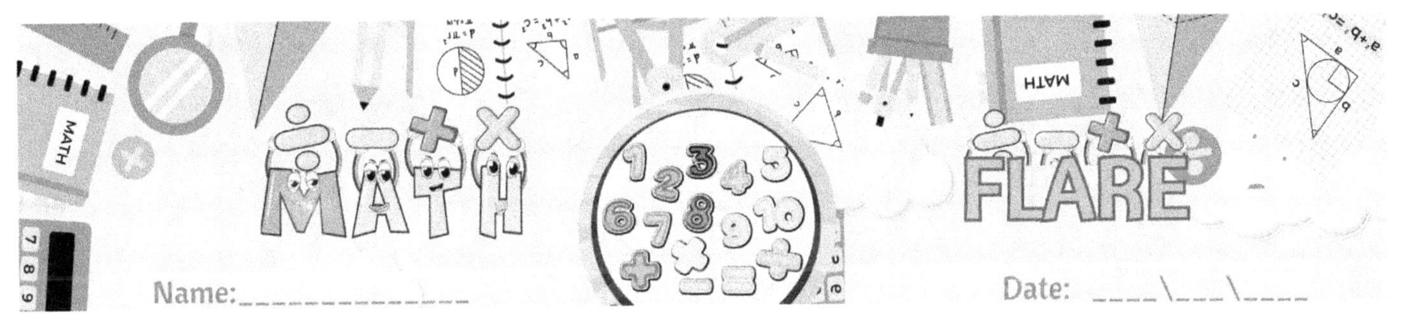

19. 17,505
   × 3,506

20. 24,405
   × 6,274

21. 86,181
   × 7,636

22. 76,461
   × 2,624

23. 38,687
   × 3,043

24. 45,538
   × 9,262

25. 88,554
   × 5,120

26. 80,324
   × 2,544

27. 38,706
   × 3,092

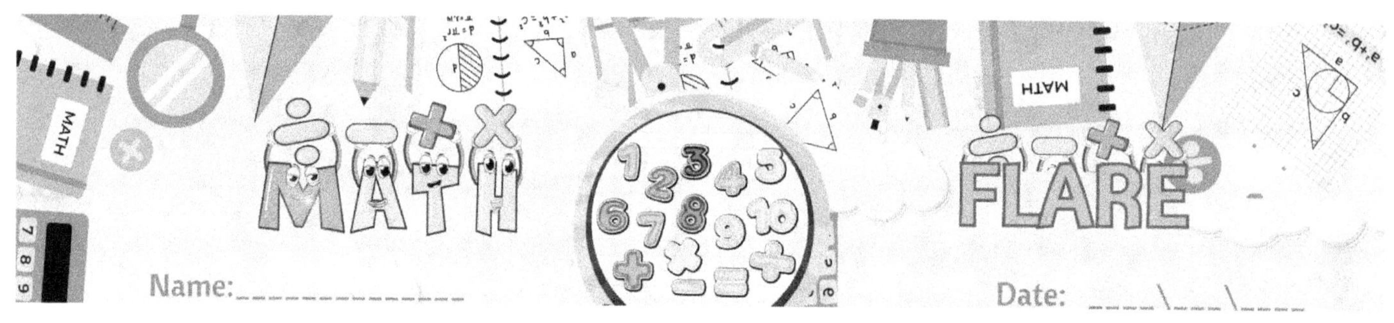

28. 86,126 × 3,270	29. 47,534 × 5,251	30. 14,883 × 6,863
31. 86,253 × 4,634	32. 16,461 × 9,956	33. 80,464 × 8,600
34. 89,074 × 7,389	35. 18,868 × 3,848	36. 43,502 × 7,972

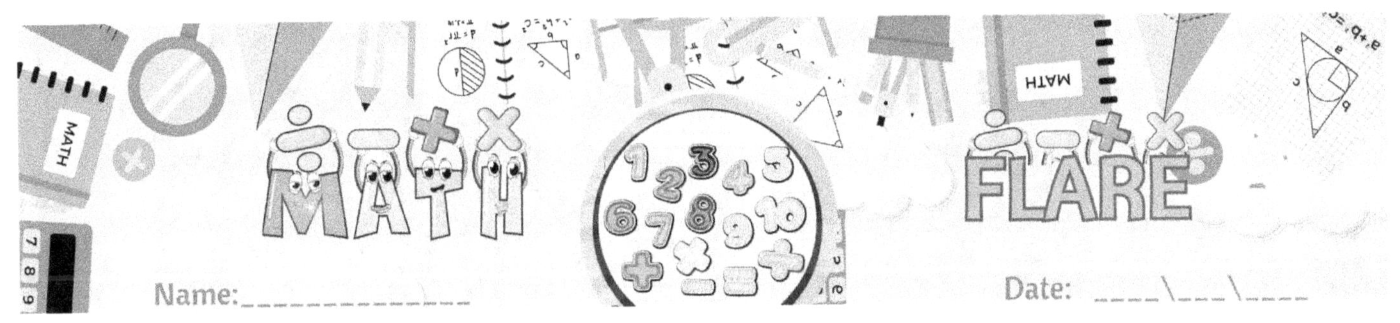

37. 64,372
   × 7,144

38. 43,650
   × 5,146

39. 83,929
   × 8,411

40. 50,119
   × 1,560

41. 67,301
   × 2,793

42. 15,424
   × 4,958

43. 58,333
   × 4,759

44. 89,685
   × 2,965

45. 87,462
   × 3,168

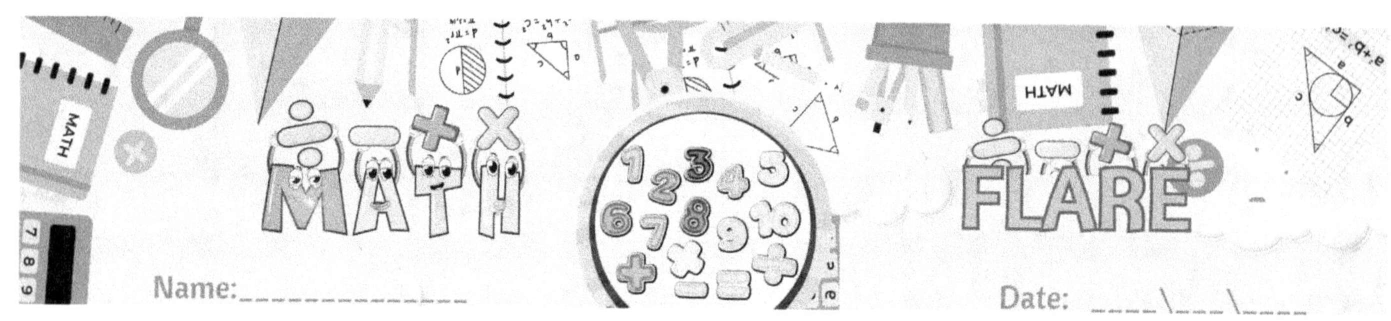

46. 28,343
   × 6,498

47. 30,177
   × 5,577

48. 76,473
   × 4,984

49. 69,895
   × 7,689

50. 45,770
   × 5,268

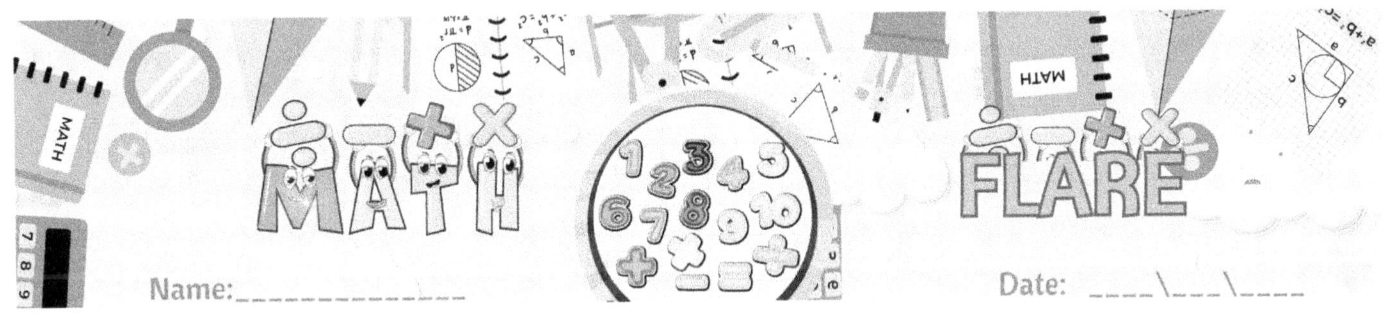

Long Division
Find the quotient.

51.

$$5 \overline{) 711{,}790}$$

52.

$$9 \overline{) 312{,}444}$$

53.

$$17 \overline{) 246{,}508}$$

54.

$$17 \overline{) 919{,}774}$$

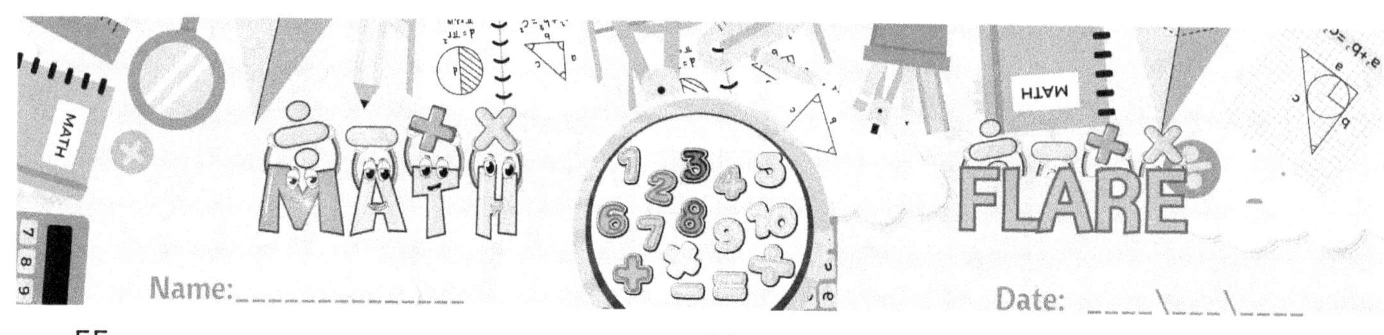

55.

$$16\overline{)310{,}898}$$

56.

$$20\overline{)795{,}027}$$

57.

$$5\overline{)178{,}728}$$

58.

$$17\overline{)661{,}200}$$

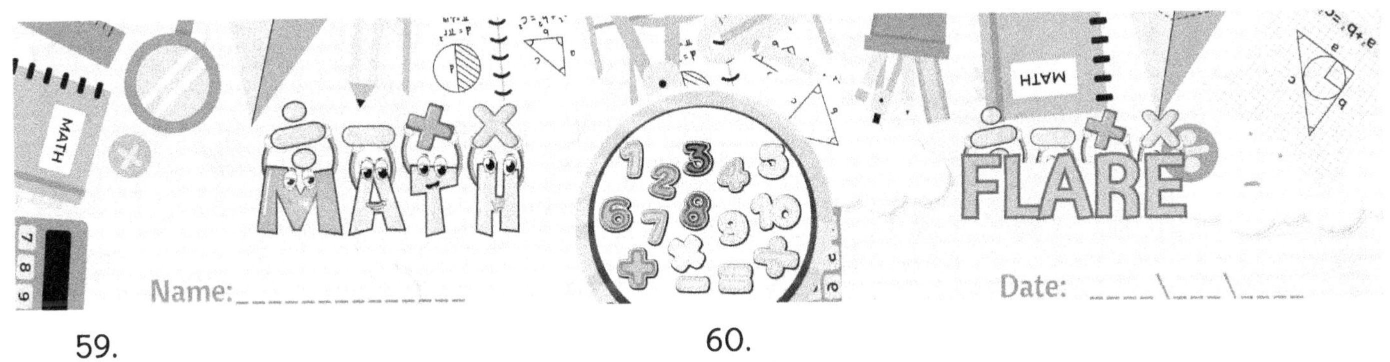

59.

$$13\overline{)228{,}893}$$

60.

$$6\overline{)777{,}614}$$

61.

$$12\overline{)989{,}900}$$

62.

$$11\overline{)669{,}958}$$

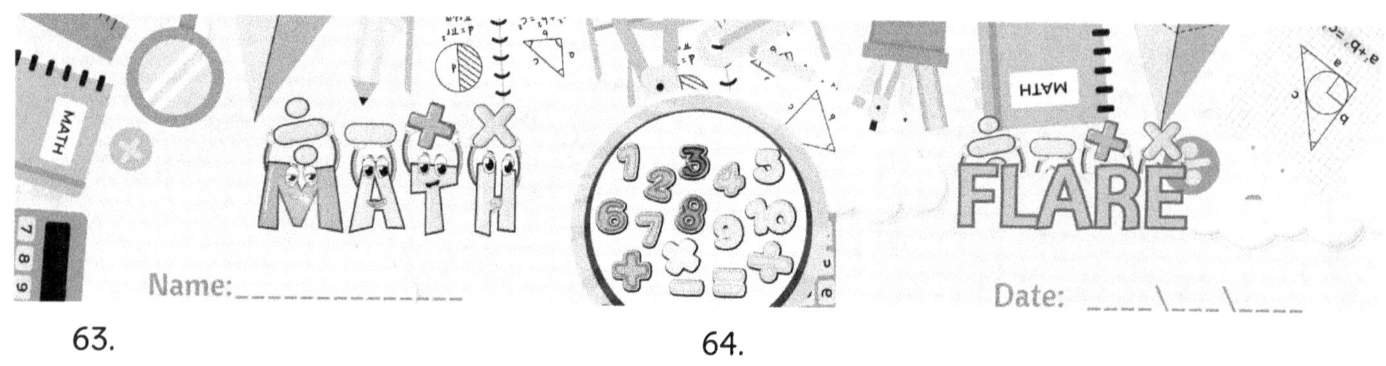

63.

$$4 \overline{)\ 805{,}106}$$

64.

$$15 \overline{)\ 110{,}756}$$

65.

$$8 \overline{)\ 485{,}583}$$

66.

$$9 \overline{)\ 271{,}791}$$

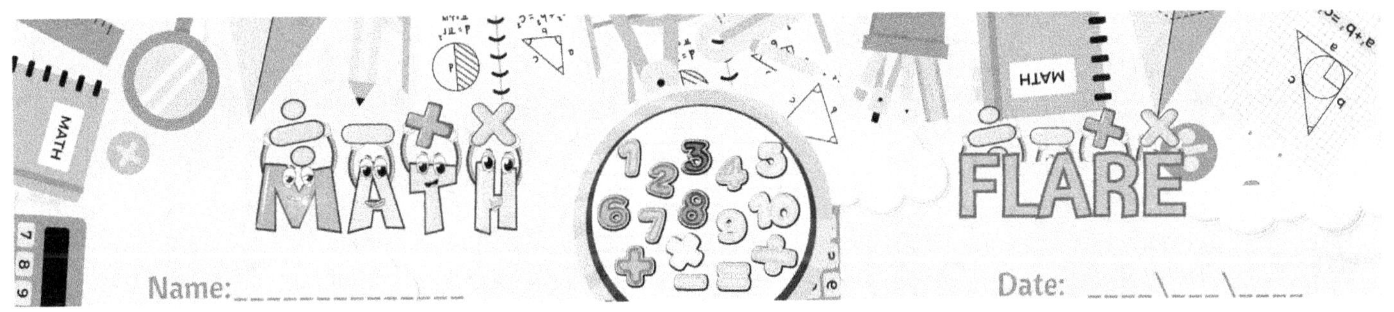

67.

11$\overline{)953,873}$

68.

5$\overline{)651,908}$

69.

20$\overline{)483,117}$

70.

17$\overline{)779,350}$

71.

$$15\overline{)571{,}576}$$

72.

$$18\overline{)276{,}906}$$

73.

$$15\overline{)656{,}146}$$

74.

$$11\overline{)618{,}054}$$

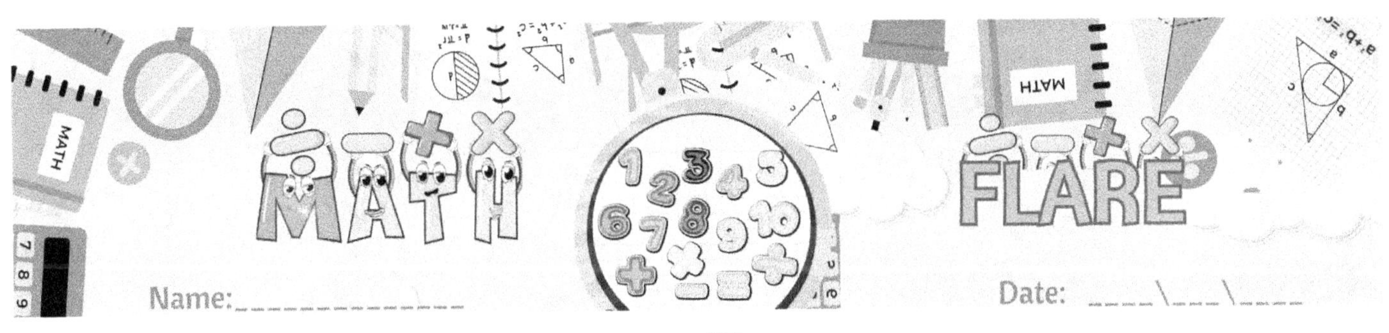

Name:______________   Date: ____________

75.

$7 \overline{)493,144}$

76.

$8 \overline{)418,761}$

77.

$16 \overline{)768,621}$

78.

$4 \overline{)217,309}$

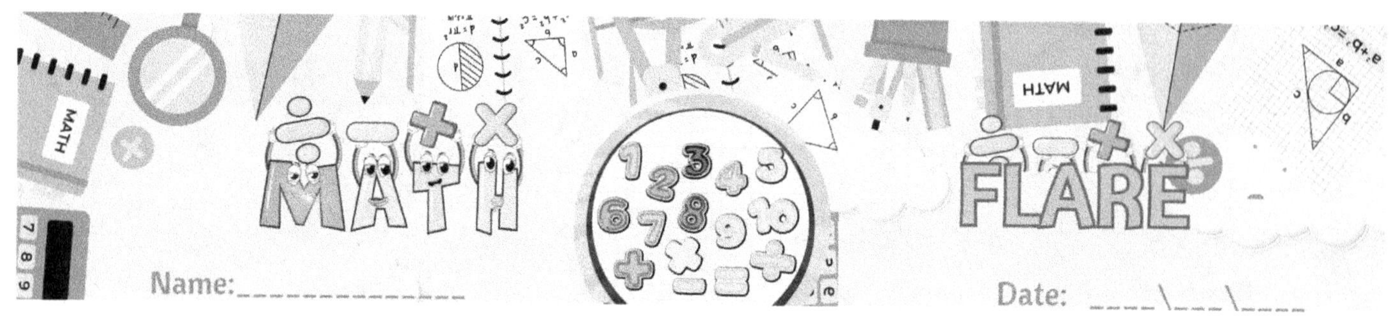

Long Division: Remainders

Find the quotient.

79.

$48 \overline{)\,477{,}281}$

80.

$16 \overline{)\,144{,}205}$

81.

$20 \overline{)\,667{,}692}$

82.

$38 \overline{)\,452{,}816}$

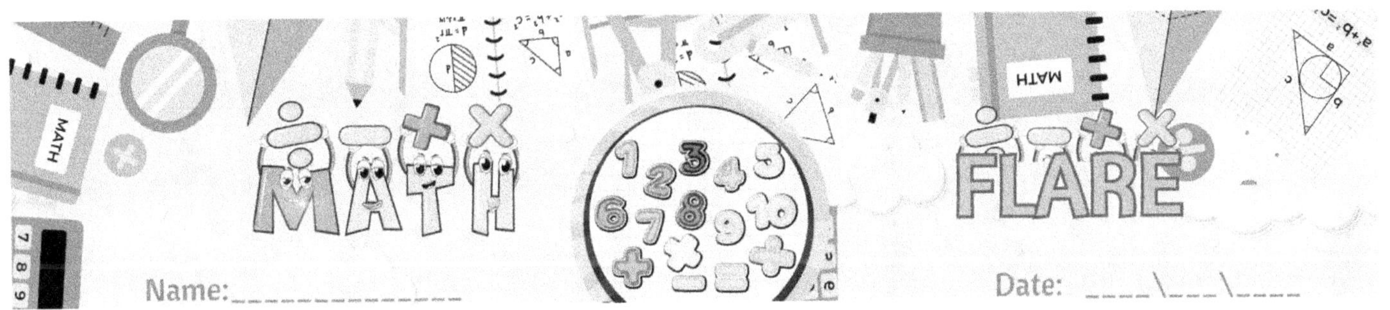

83.

$$33 \overline{)\ 787{,}415}$$

84.

$$48 \overline{)\ 919{,}188}$$

85.

$$48 \overline{)\ 488{,}177}$$

86.

$$39 \overline{)\ 250{,}173}$$

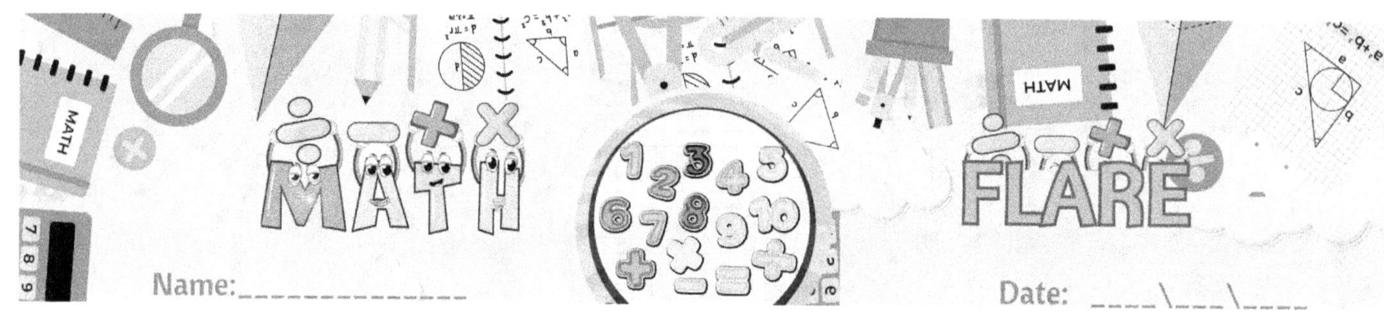

87.

$$13 \overline{)639,228}$$

88.

$$30 \overline{)401,406}$$

89.

$$39 \overline{)134,001}$$

90.

$$26 \overline{)281,216}$$

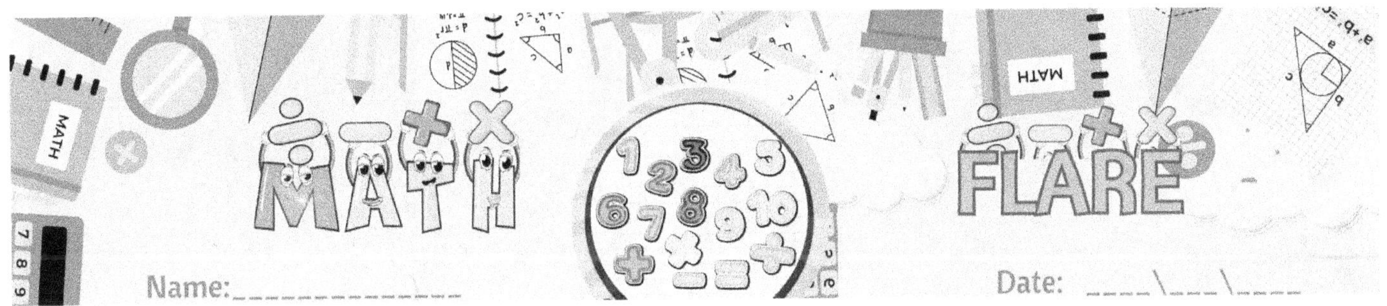

91.

22) 574,381

92.

46) 149,175

93.

37) 973,720

94.

34) 156,366

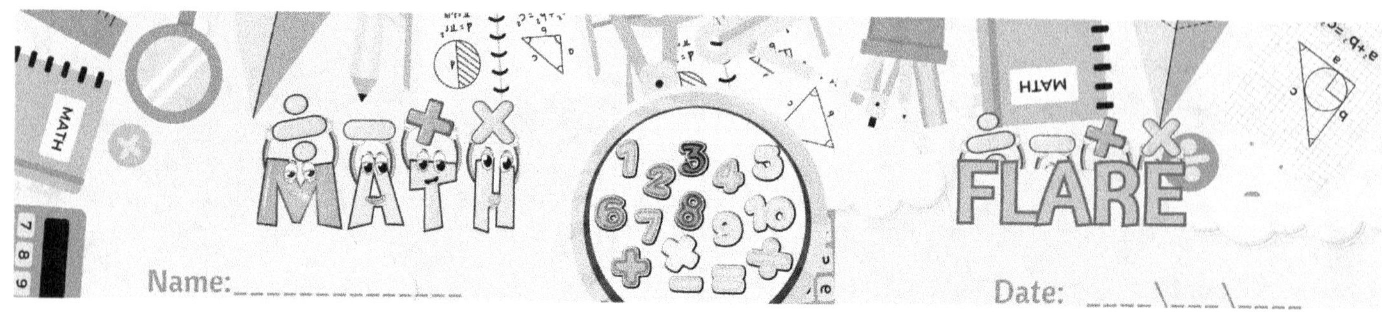

95.

$$49 \overline{)\, 571{,}374}$$

96.

$$24 \overline{)\, 919{,}478}$$

97.

$$49 \overline{)\, 709{,}014}$$

98.

$$29 \overline{)\, 295{,}007}$$

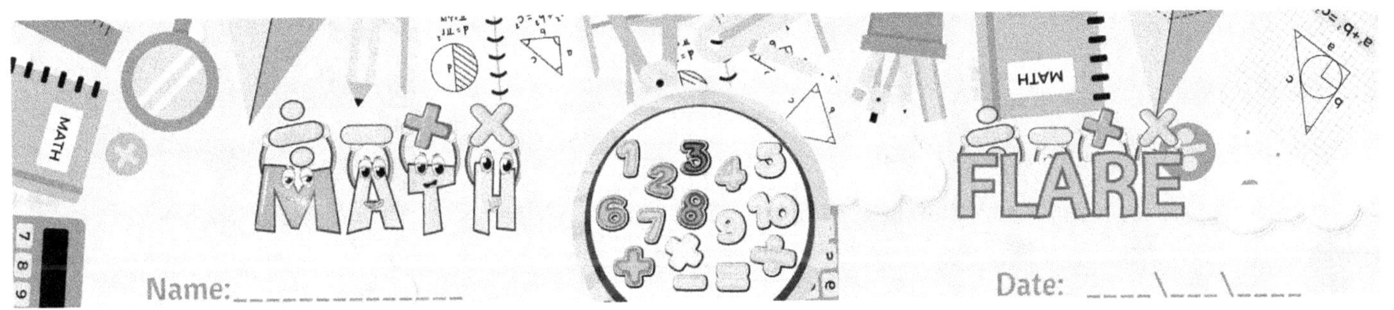

99.

$$46 \overline{)\ 214{,}363}$$

100.

$$46 \overline{)\ 692{,}396}$$

101.

$$27 \overline{)\ 867{,}059}$$

102.

$$45 \overline{)\ 667{,}257}$$

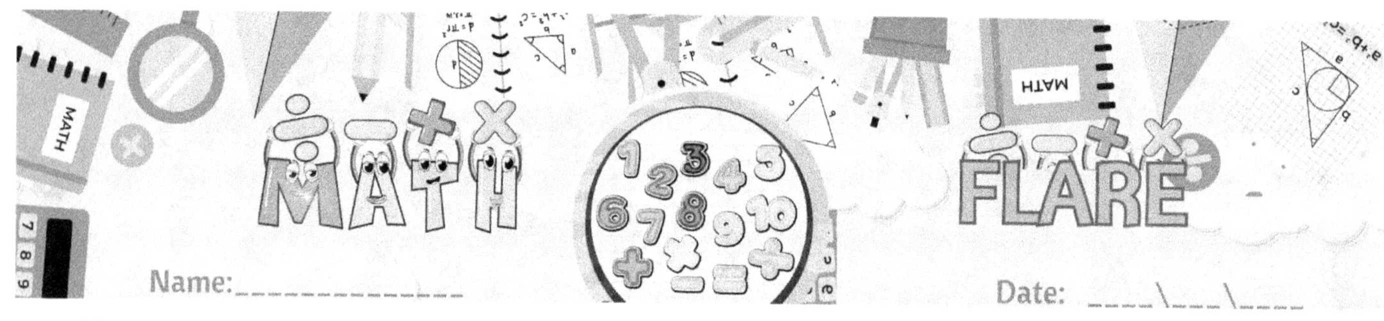

103.

$$41 \overline{)749{,}958}$$

104.

$$23 \overline{)673{,}261}$$

105.

$$27 \overline{)281{,}457}$$

106.

$$38 \overline{)697{,}625}$$

Name:_________________

Date: ___________

107.

$$36\overline{)782,706}$$

108.

$$24\overline{)661,174}$$

109.

$$29\overline{)279,378}$$

110.

$$14\overline{)766,154}$$

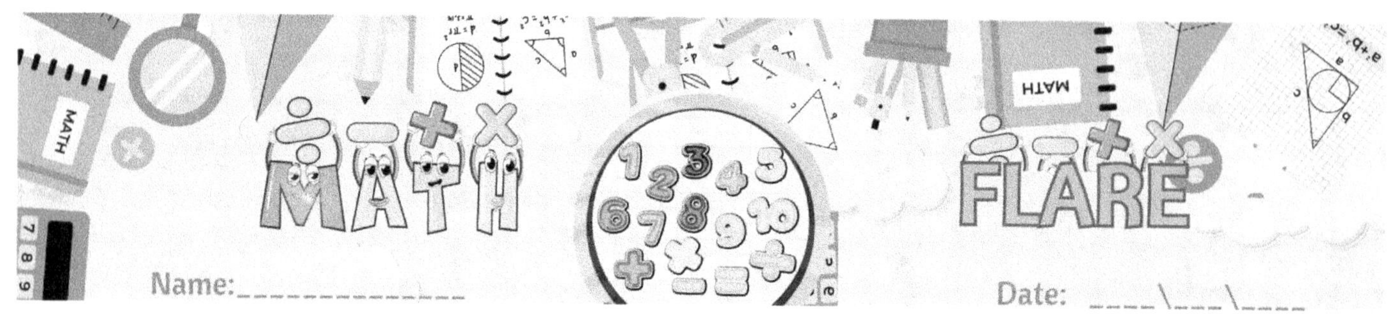

111.

$$23\overline{)568{,}024}$$

112.

$$28\overline{)479{,}190}$$

113.

$$43\overline{)131{,}752}$$

114.

$$35\overline{)136{,}274}$$

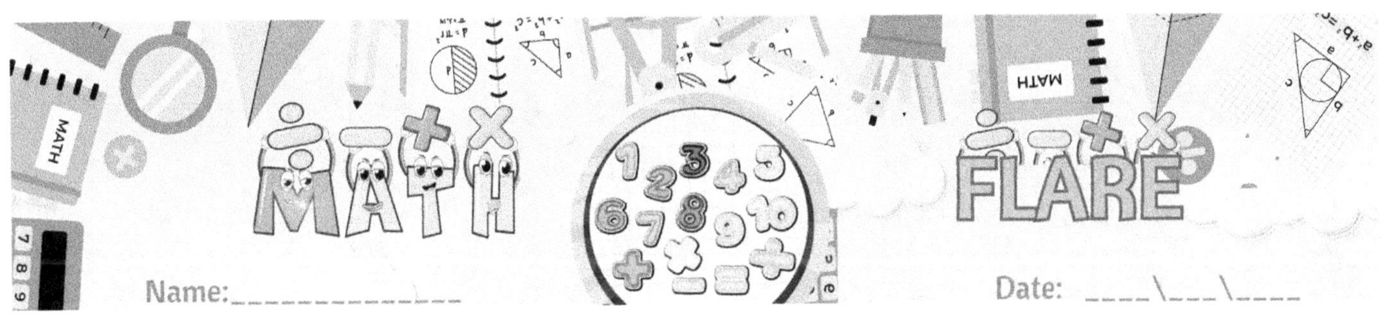

115.

45) 876,311

116.

15) 437,973

117.

22) 162,463

118.

14) 599,019

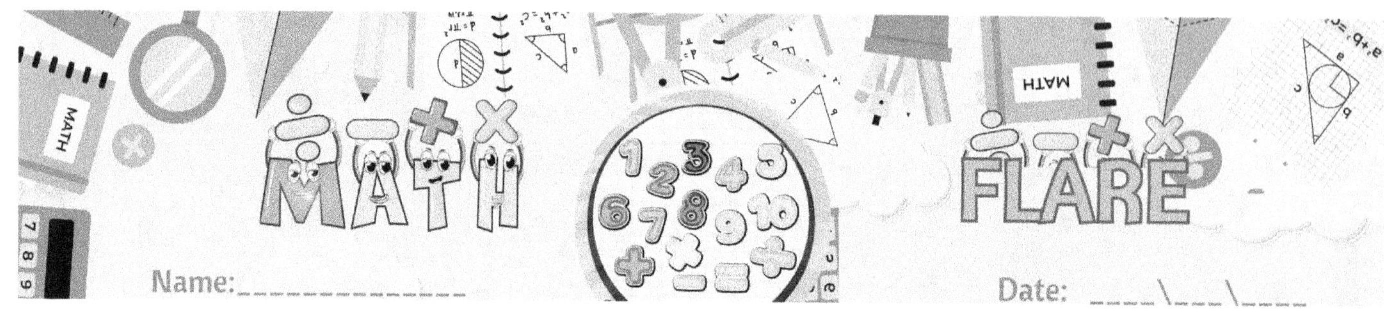

119.

$$17 \overline{)\, 691,636}$$

120.

$$18 \overline{)\, 268,122}$$

121.

$$40 \overline{)\, 130,867}$$

122.

$$14 \overline{)\, 447,433}$$

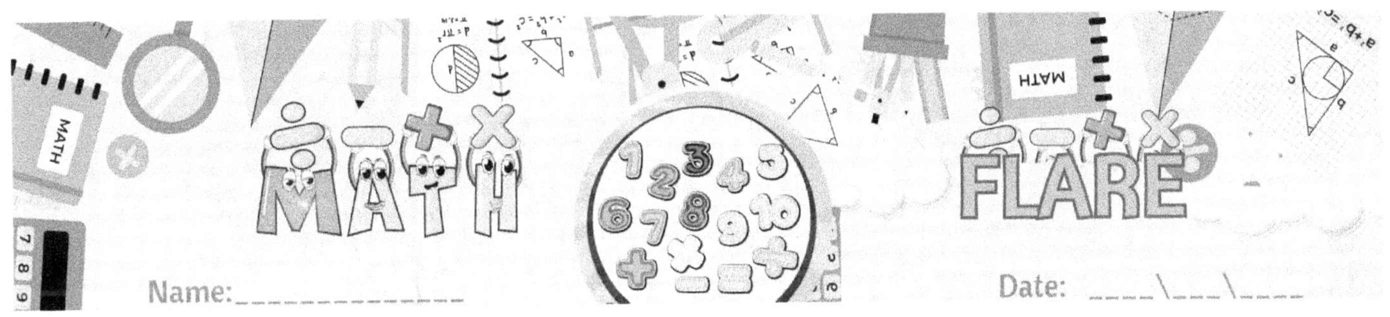

123.

$$19 \overline{)\ 386{,}250}$$

124.

$$11 \overline{)\ 628{,}757}$$

125.

$$45 \overline{)\ 411{,}526}$$

126.

$$36 \overline{)\ 344{,}433}$$

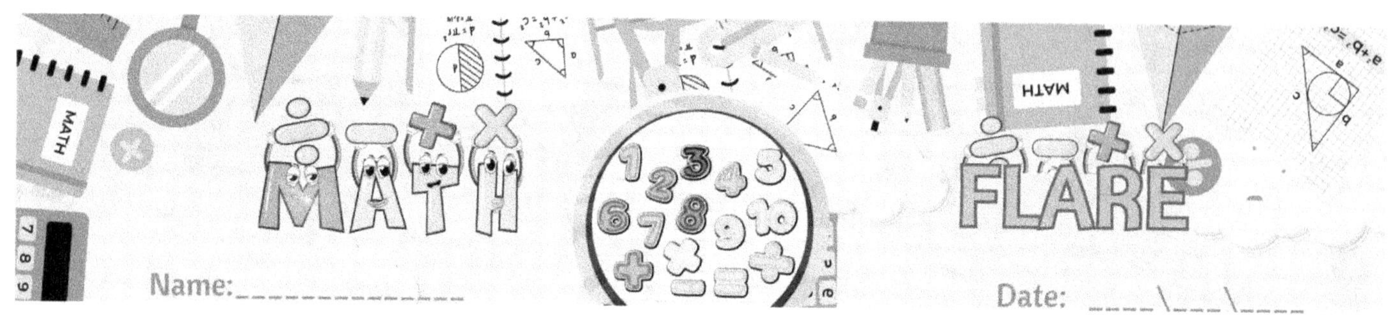

127.

33) 245,130

128.

31) 435,837

129.

17) 109,527

130.

46) 853,463

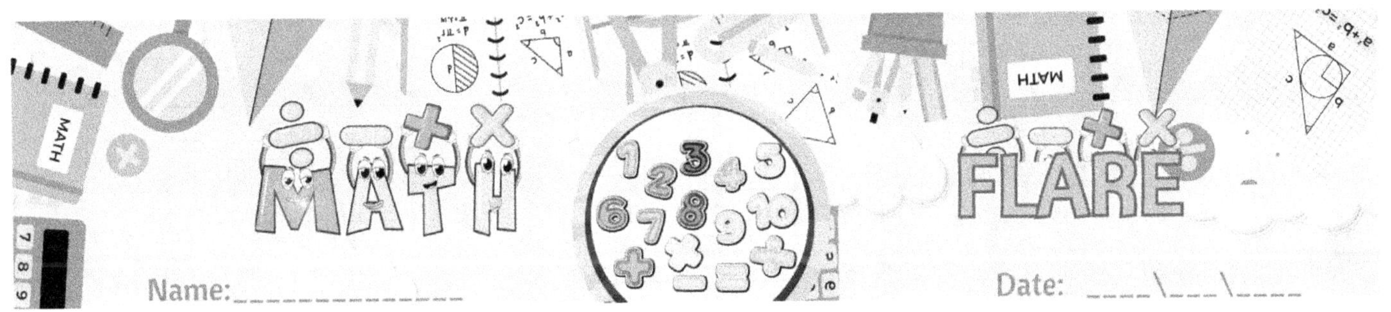

Name:_______________

Date: _____ ____ ____

131.

$$10 \overline{)\ 767,432}$$

132.

$$24 \overline{)\ 511,449}$$

133.

$$31 \overline{)\ 150,616}$$

134.

$$28 \overline{)\ 659,958}$$

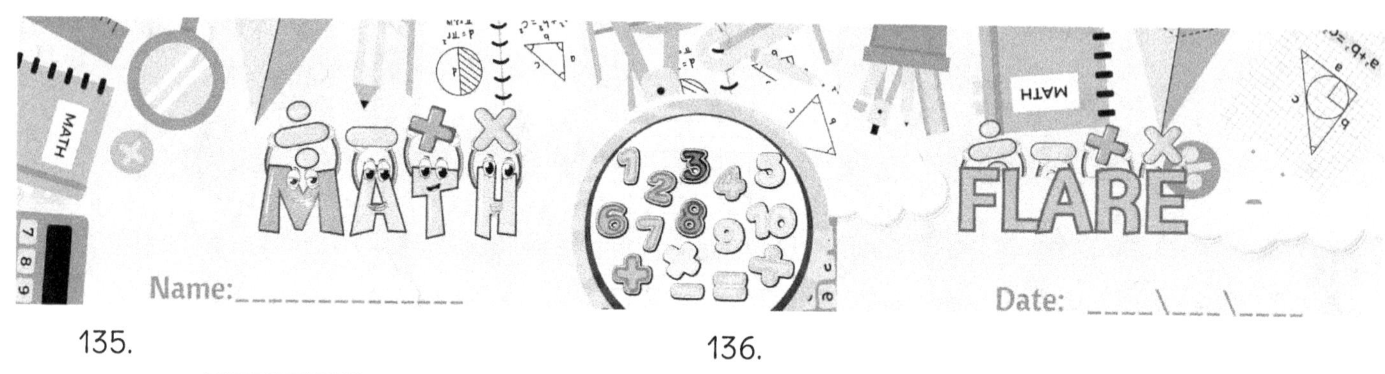

Name:_______________

Date: _______________

135.

$$31 \overline{)\ 179{,}107}$$

136.

$$11 \overline{)\ 717{,}161}$$

137.

$$32 \overline{)\ 366{,}614}$$

138.

$$41 \overline{)\ 152{,}421}$$

139.

$$23 \overline{)\, 942{,}864}$$

140.

$$43 \overline{)\, 218{,}052}$$

141.

$$10 \overline{)\, 309{,}952}$$

142.

$$50 \overline{)\, 355{,}000}$$

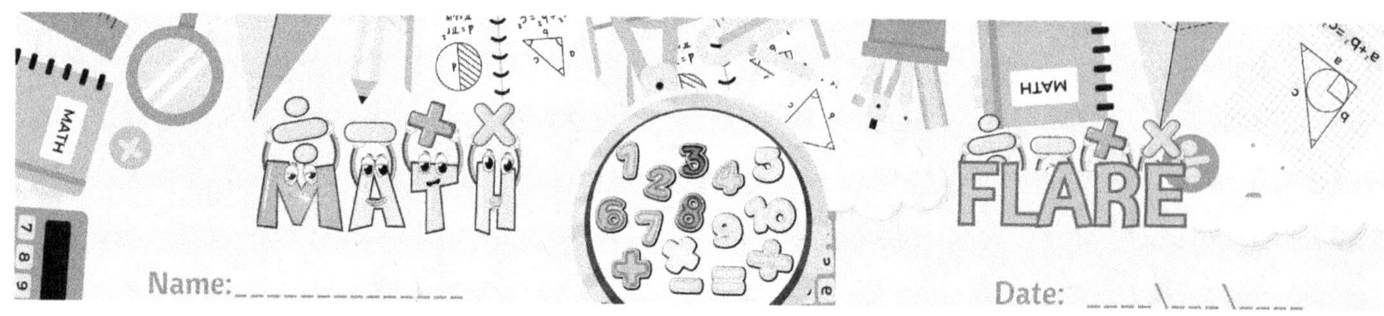

143.

$$39 \overline{)633{,}160}$$

144.

$$30 \overline{)977{,}585}$$

145.

$$11 \overline{)941{,}517}$$

146.

$$29 \overline{)176{,}137}$$

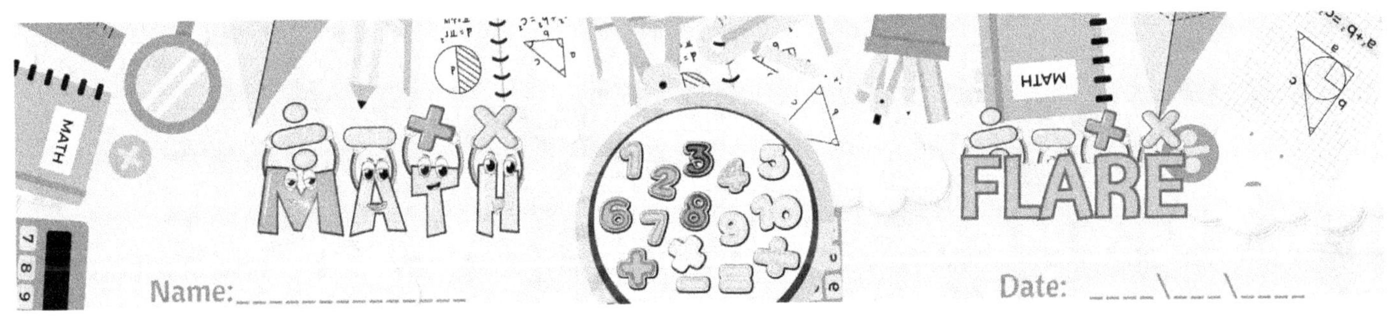

147.

$$21\overline{)410{,}495}$$

148.

$$11\overline{)502{,}581}$$

149.

$$12\overline{)357{,}156}$$

150.

$$42\overline{)132{,}170}$$

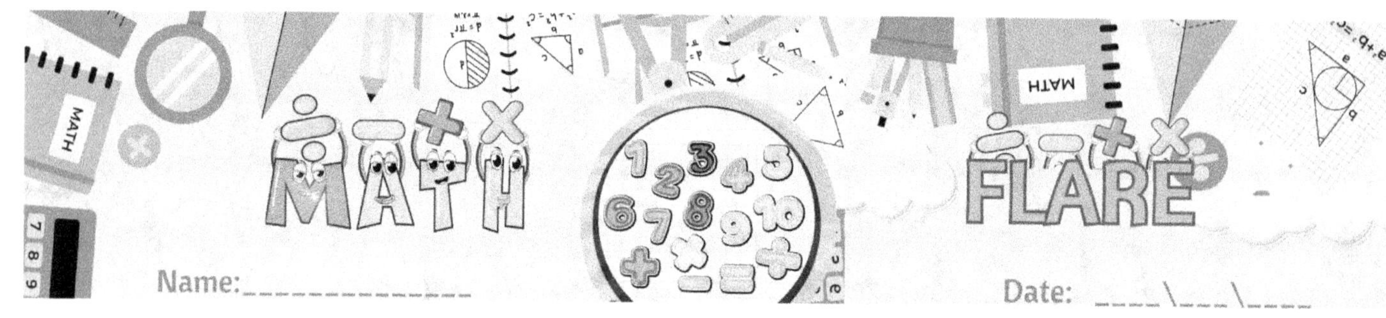

151.

$$15 \overline{)637,099}$$

152.

$$43 \overline{)951,781}$$

153.

$$20 \overline{)269,048}$$

154.

$$34 \overline{)413,012}$$

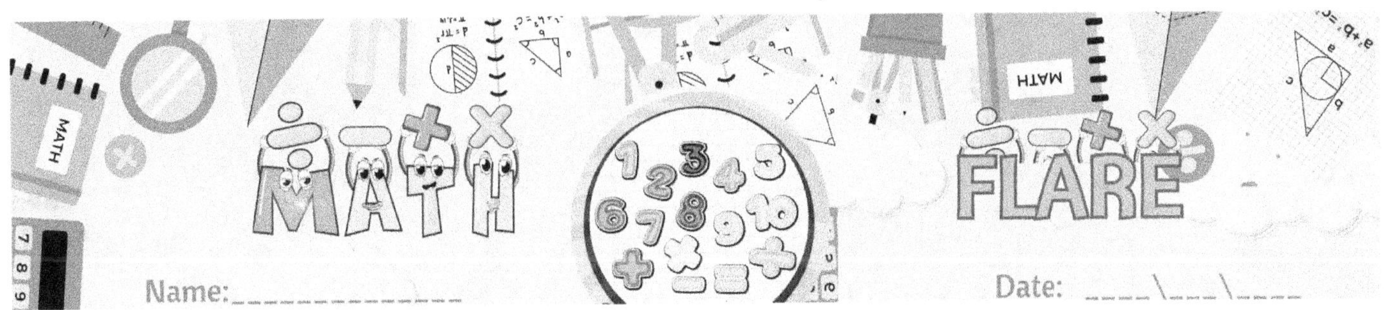

155.

$34 \overline{)556{,}688}$

156.

$37 \overline{)633{,}896}$

157.

$11 \overline{)144{,}904}$

158.

$39 \overline{)701{,}297}$

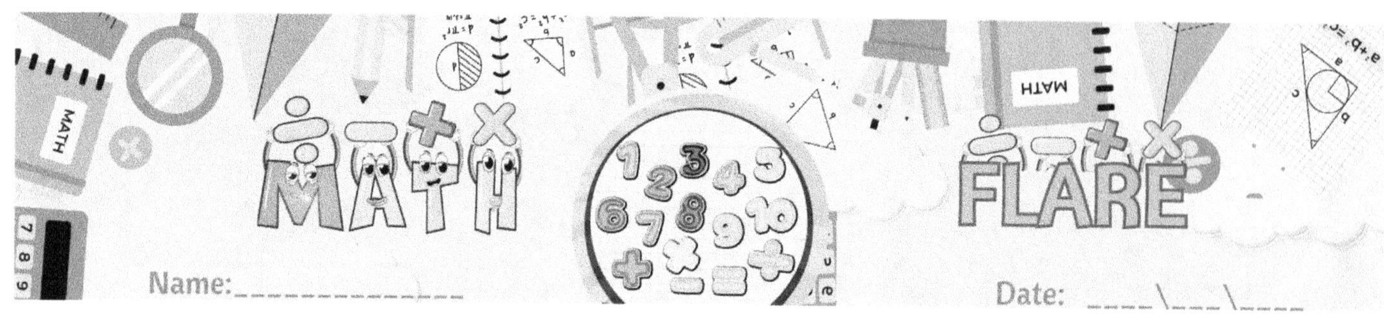

159.

$$29\overline{)751{,}732}$$

160.

$$23\overline{)770{,}701}$$

161.

$$15\overline{)597{,}323}$$

162.

$$13\overline{)563{,}834}$$

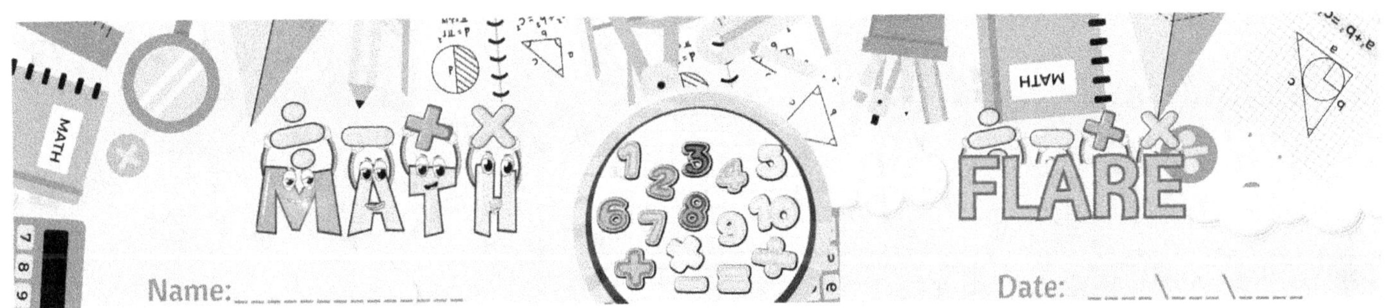

163.

$$18\overline{)499{,}373}$$

164.

$$10\overline{)704{,}923}$$

165.

$$11\overline{)193{,}560}$$

166.

$$46\overline{)542{,}263}$$

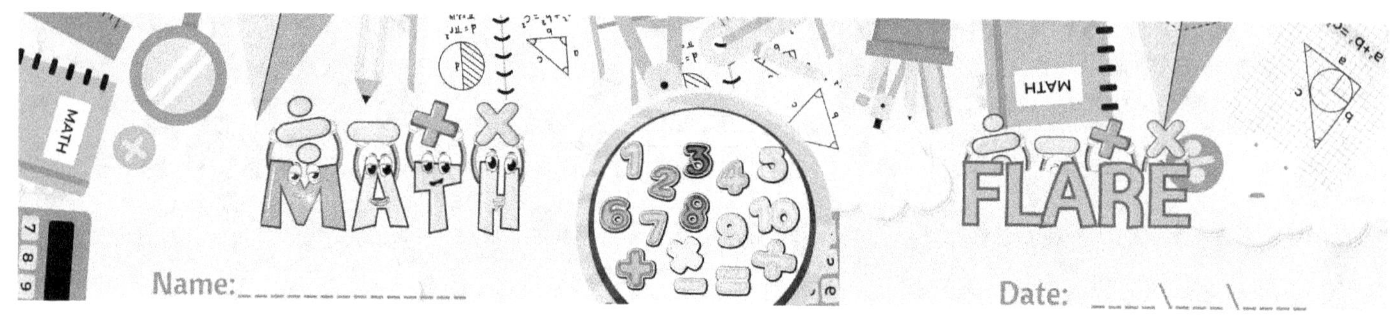

167.

24) 364,235

168.

14) 297,595

169.

29) 153,604

170.

24) 821,054

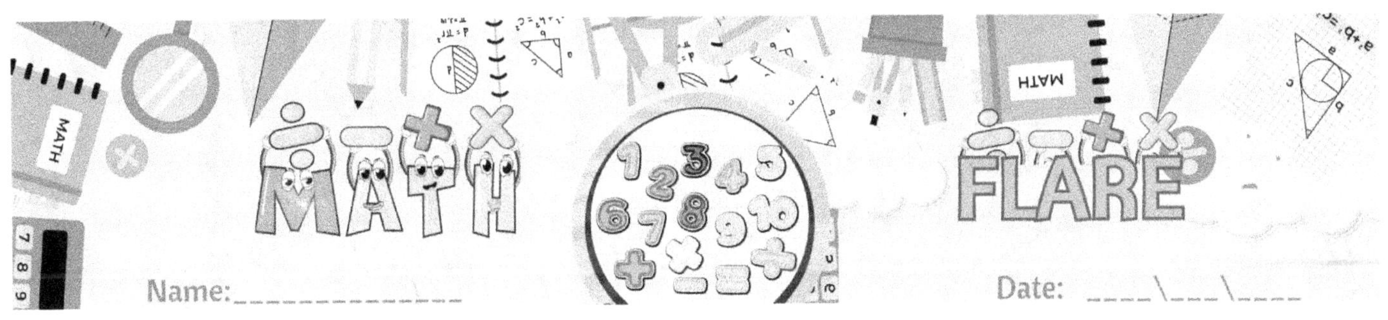

171.

$$25 \overline{)\,445{,}333}$$

172.

$$24 \overline{)\,996{,}665}$$

173.

$$26 \overline{)\,488{,}361}$$

174.

$$23 \overline{)\,483{,}777}$$

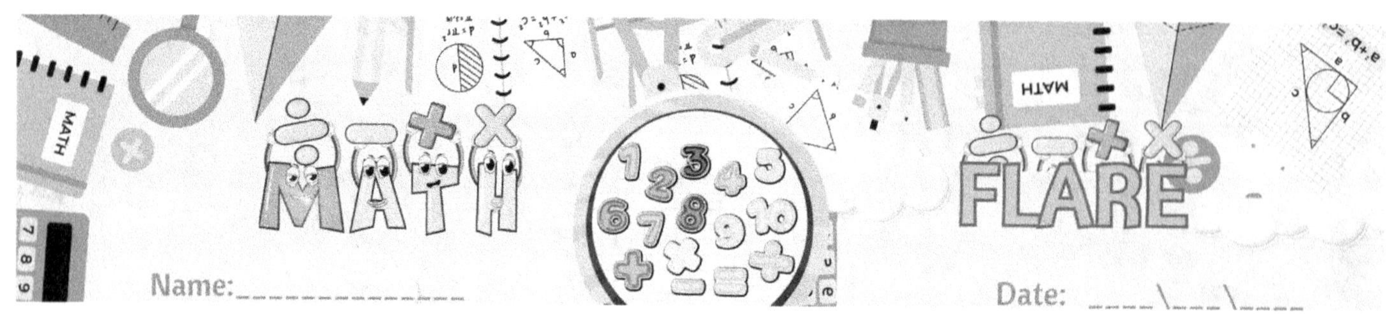

175.

$$38 \overline{)655{,}574}$$

176.

$$43 \overline{)372{,}399}$$

177.

$$38 \overline{)372{,}869}$$

178.

$$29 \overline{)314{,}017}$$

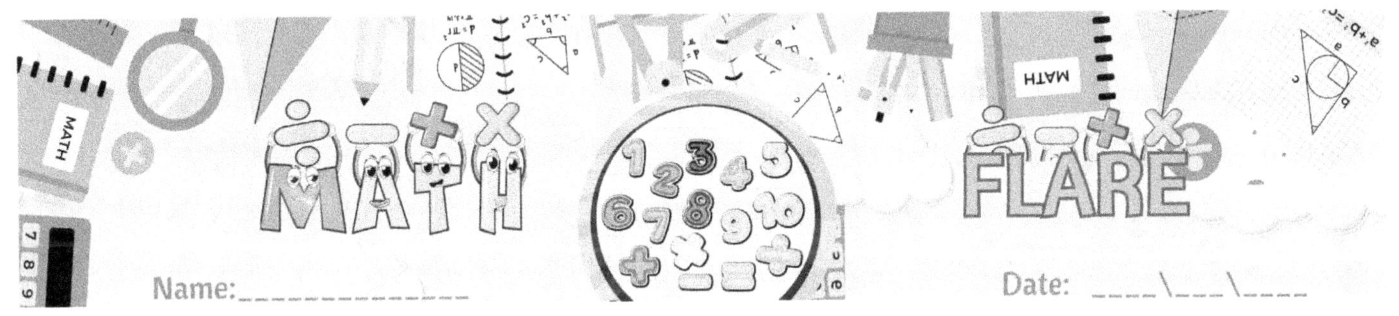

Using the Power of 10

179.
$$\begin{array}{r} 1{,}000 \\ \times\ \ \ \ 100 \\ \hline \end{array}$$

180.
$$\begin{array}{r} 2{,}000 \\ \times\ \ \ \ \ \ 10 \\ \hline \end{array}$$

181.
$$\begin{array}{r} 1{,}000 \\ \times\ 1{,}000 \\ \hline \end{array}$$

182.
$$\begin{array}{r} 2{,}000 \\ \times\ 1{,}000 \\ \hline \end{array}$$

183.
$$\begin{array}{r} 9{,}000 \\ \times\ \ \ \ \ 0.1 \\ \hline \end{array}$$

184.
$$1{,}000\overline{)4{,}000}$$

185.
$$\begin{array}{r} 1{,}000 \\ \times\ \ \ \ 100 \\ \hline \end{array}$$

186.
$$0.001\overline{)5{,}000}$$

187.
$$\begin{array}{r} 2{,}000 \\ \times\ \ \ 0.01 \\ \hline \end{array}$$

188.
$$\begin{array}{r} 1{,}000 \\ \times\ \ \ 0.01 \\ \hline \end{array}$$

189.
$$0.001\overline{)2{,}000}$$

190.
$$10\overline{)9{,}000}$$

191.   3,000
     × 0.001

192.   100⟌7,000

193.   9,000
     × 1,000

194.   1,000
     ×   10

195.   3,000
     × 0.001

196.   1,000
     ×   0.1

197.   1,000⟌5,000

198.   0.01⟌9,000

199.   0.01⟌9,000

200.   0.01⟌7,000

201.   10⟌1,000

202.   0.001⟌3,000

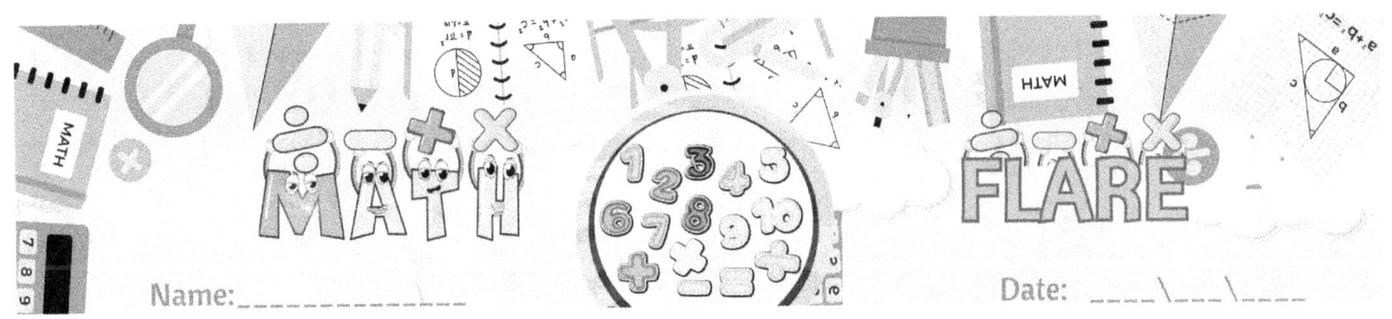

Name:____________________

Date: ____________

203.
$$6{,}000 \times 10$$

204.
$$2{,}000 \times 100$$

205.
$$1{,}000 \overline{)\,3{,}000}$$

206.
$$2{,}000 \times 10$$

207.
$$6{,}000 \times 0.1$$

208.
$$100 \overline{)\,4{,}000}$$

209.
$$10 \overline{)\,6{,}000}$$

210.
$$0.01 \overline{)\,5{,}000}$$

211.
$$8{,}000 \times 0.1$$

212.
$$10 \overline{)\,4{,}000}$$

213.
$$1{,}000 \overline{)\,2{,}000}$$

214.
$$1{,}000 \overline{)\,3{,}000}$$

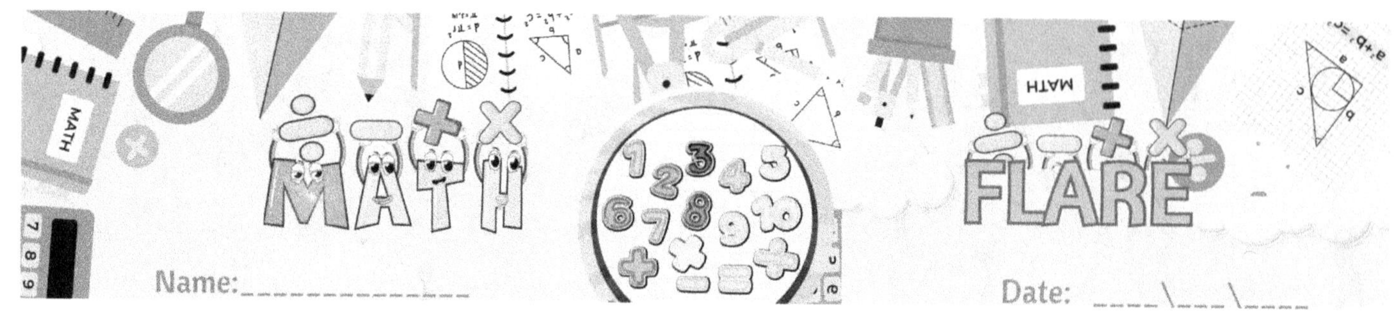

215.

$$0.01 \overline{)\ 8{,}000}$$

216.

$$100 \overline{)\ 2{,}000}$$

217.

$$0.001 \overline{)\ 7{,}000}$$

218.

$$\begin{array}{r} 2{,}000 \\ \times\quad 0.01 \\ \hline \end{array}$$

219.

$$\begin{array}{r} 5{,}000 \\ \times\quad 100 \\ \hline \end{array}$$

220.

$$\begin{array}{r} 9{,}000 \\ \times\quad 0.01 \\ \hline \end{array}$$

221.

$$1{,}000 \overline{)\ 3{,}000}$$

222.

$$100 \overline{)\ 1{,}000}$$

223.

$$\begin{array}{r} 3{,}000 \\ \times\quad 0.1 \\ \hline \end{array}$$

224.

$$0.1 \overline{)\ 1{,}000}$$

225.

$$\begin{array}{r} 5{,}000 \\ \times\quad 10 \\ \hline \end{array}$$

226.

$$10 \overline{)\ 2{,}000}$$

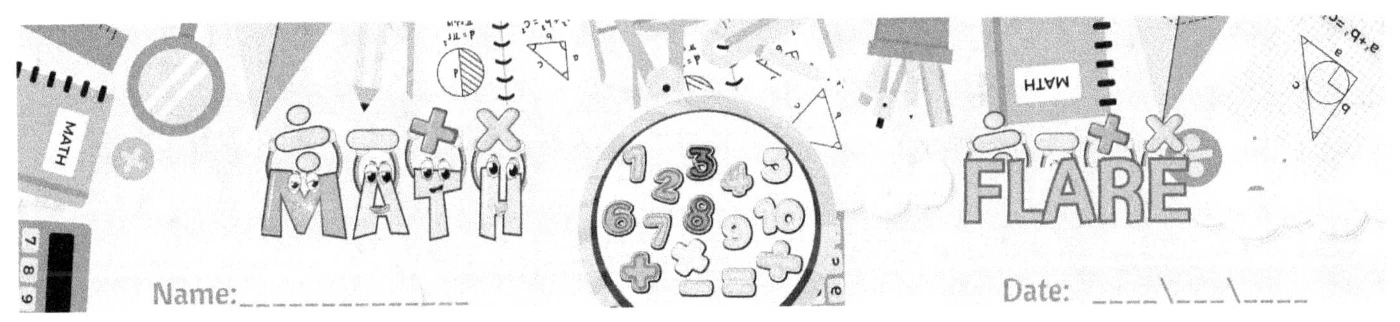

227.

$$1{,}000 \overline{)2{,}000}$$

228.

$$\begin{array}{r} 2{,}000 \\ \times \quad 0.1 \\ \hline \end{array}$$

229.

$$\begin{array}{r} 4{,}000 \\ \times \quad 0.001 \\ \hline \end{array}$$

230.

$$0.01 \overline{)7{,}000}$$

231.

$$1{,}000 \overline{)4{,}000}$$

232.

$$\begin{array}{r} 9{,}000 \\ \times \quad 0.1 \\ \hline \end{array}$$

233.

$$0.001 \overline{)5{,}000}$$

234.

$$10 \overline{)4{,}000}$$

235.

$$\begin{array}{r} 1{,}000 \\ \times \quad 1{,}000 \\ \hline \end{array}$$

236.

$$\begin{array}{r} 8{,}000 \\ \times \quad 1{,}000 \\ \hline \end{array}$$

237.

$$\begin{array}{r} 5{,}000 \\ \times \quad 0.1 \\ \hline \end{array}$$

238.

$$\begin{array}{r} 8{,}000 \\ \times \quad 100 \\ \hline \end{array}$$

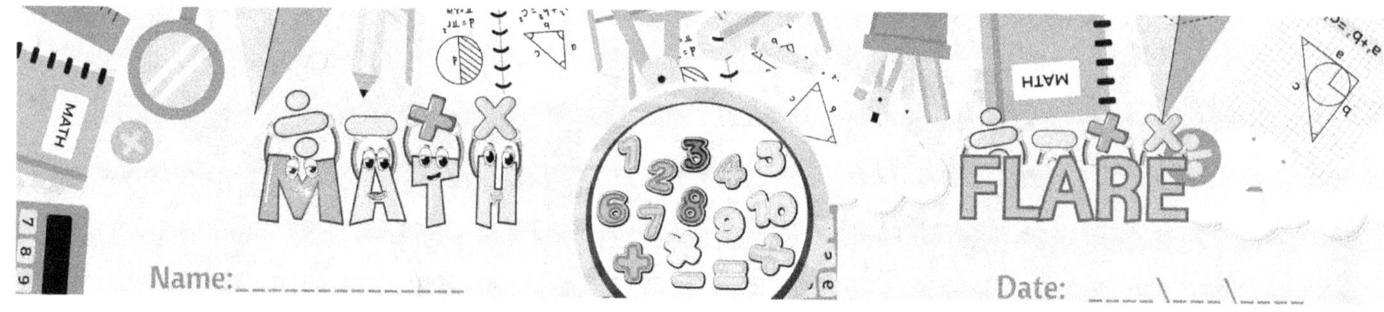

Multiplication Word Problems

239. If a bicycle travels at 20 miles per hour for 19 hours, how far will it go?

240. Parker can make seven sandwiches in 1 hour. How many sandwiches can he make in 11 hour?

241. A box contains eight bottles of juice, and each bottle contains four ounces of juice. How many ounces of juice are there in total?

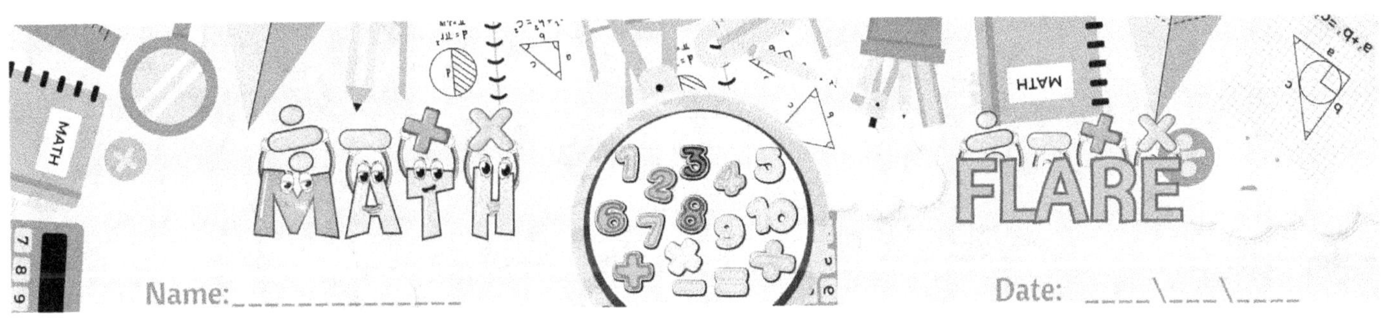

242. Claire wants to make 17 pizzas, and each pizza requires nine cups of cheese. How many cups of cheese does Claire have?

243. Caroline has five containers of paint. Each container holds 19 liters of paint. How many liters of paint does Caroline have in total?

244. Jade has 15 yards of fabric, and each dress requires 17 yards of fabric. How many dresses can Jade make?

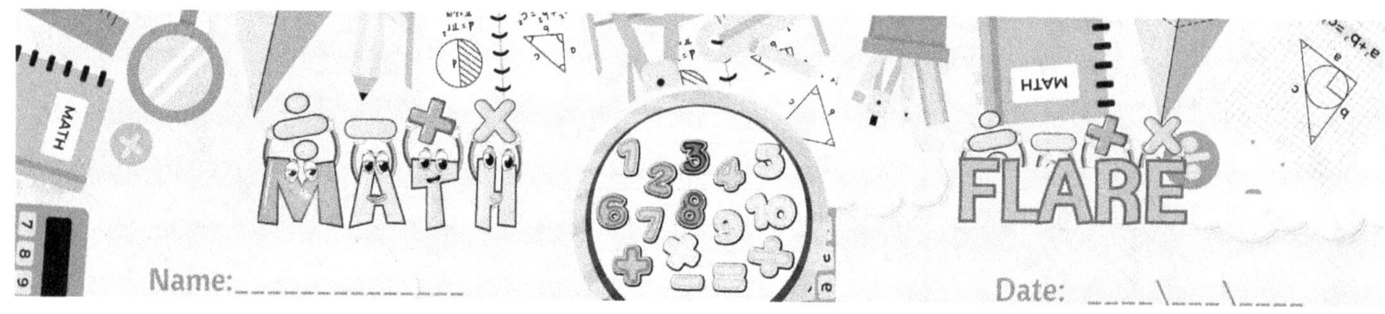

245. Dylan can do 14 pushups in one minute. How many pushups can Dylan do in seven minutes?

246. Anthony can solve 11 math problems in one hour. How many problems can Anthony solve in 18 hours?

247. There are 14 cars in a parking lot. If each car needs five liters of gasoline, how many liters of gasoline are needed for all the cars?

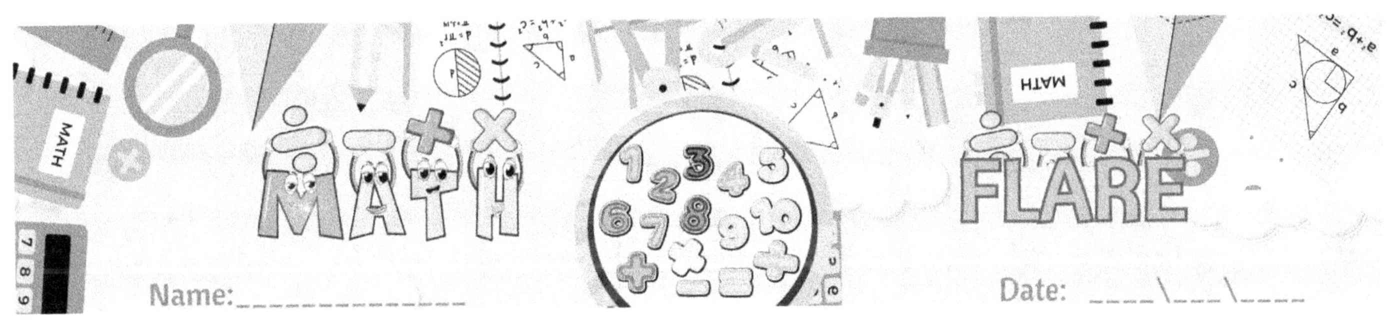

248. Jace can lift nine pounds of weight. How many pounds of weight can Jace lift in total if he lifts for 17 sets?

249. Aurora has 20 books. Each book has 17 pages. How many pages does Aurora have in all?

250. There are seven pencils in each pack. If Lydia buys 20 packs, how many pencils will Lydia have?

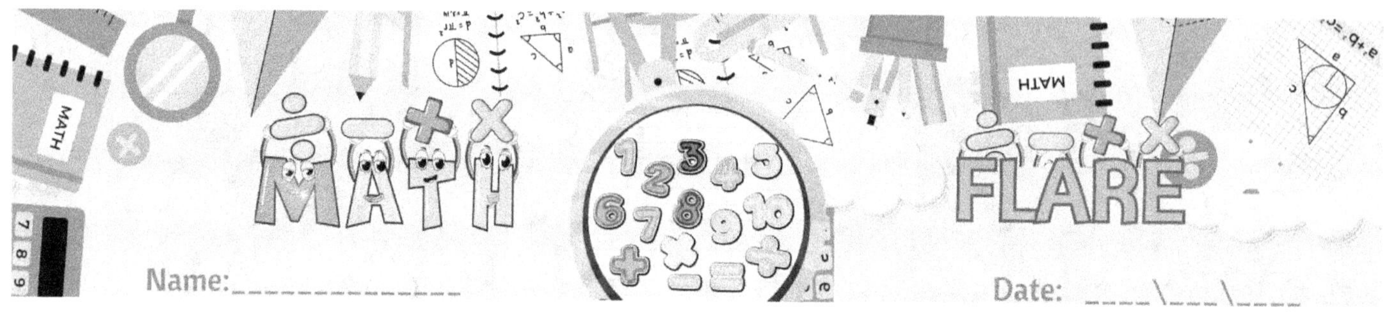

251. Scarlett has seven jars of jam. Each jar has 16 ounces of jam. How many ounces of jam does Scarlett have in all?

252. Genesis baked 16 batches of cakes. Each batch had three cakes. How many cakes did Genesis bake in all?

253. Ian can type 14 words per minute. How many words can Ian type in 13 minutes?

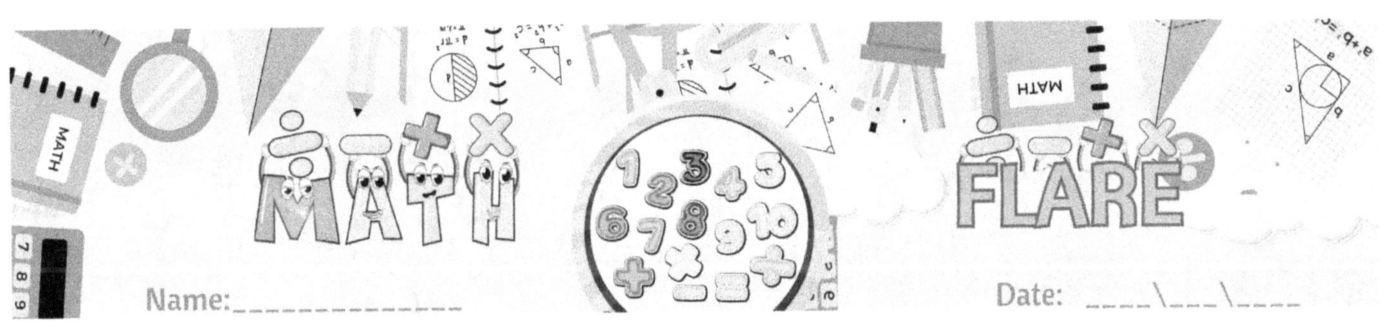

254. Bella baked two batches of cookies. Each batch had 13 cookies. How many cookies did Bella bake in all?

255. There are 13 shelves in Cooper's bookcase. 13 books can fit on each shelf. How many books can the bookcase hold in total?

256. Ryder runs 17 miles per week. How many miles will Ryder run in seven weeks?

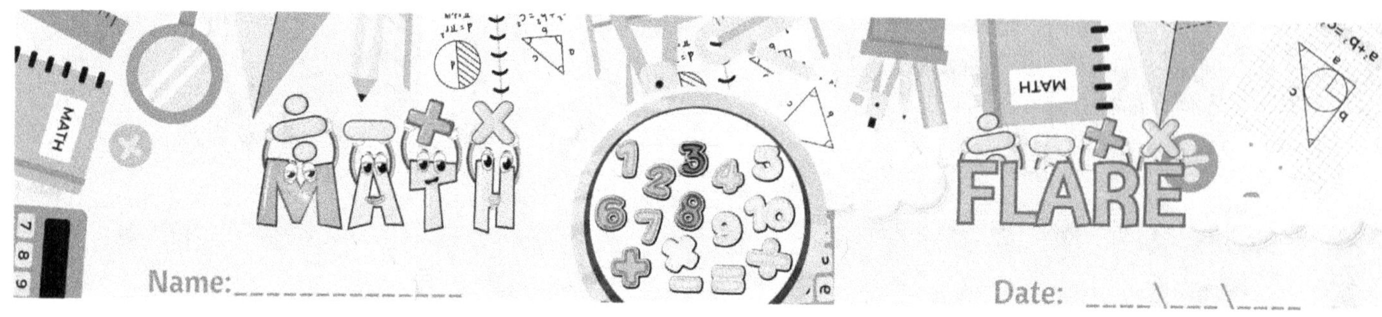

257. Gabriel sells 12 cakes each day at his bakery. If he works 12 days, how many cakes does he sell?

258. There are 17 pages in a book. If nine books are needed for a class, how many pages are there in total?

259. Benjamin can solve 17 math problems in one hour. How many math problems can Benjamin solve in 20 hours?

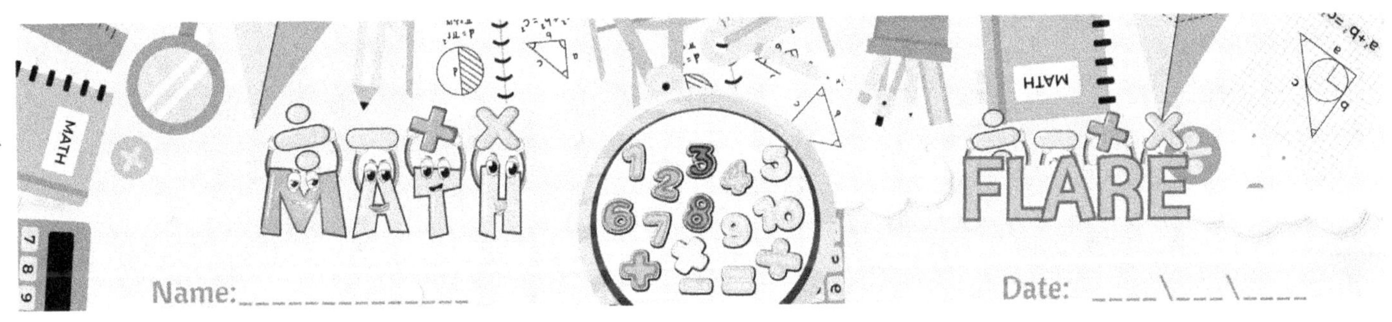

260. There are four cups in each bag. If Peyton buys four bags, how many cups will Peyton have?

261. A garden has 20 rows of flowers and three flowers in each row. How many flowers are there in total?

262. If a boat travels at two miles per hour for 17 hours, how far will it go?

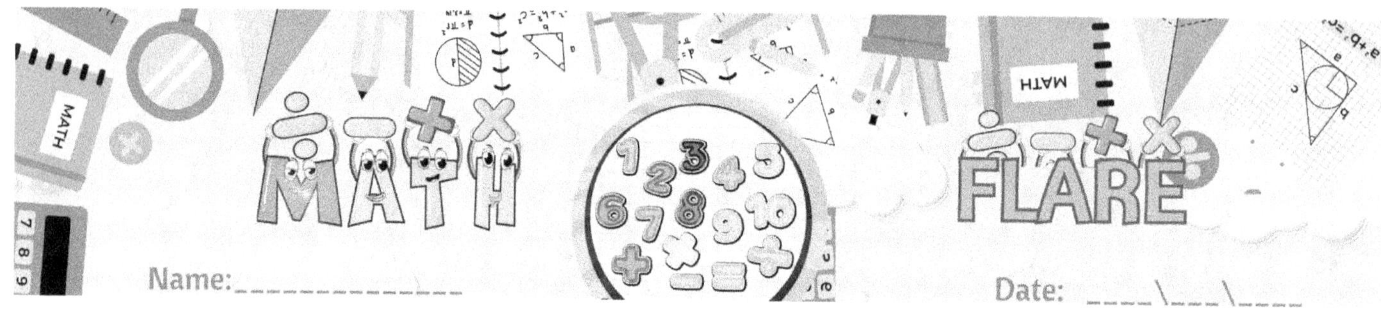

263. If a car travels at 20 miles per hour for 20 hours, how far will it go?

264. A movie theater can seat 17 people. How many people can it seat in 19 showings?

265. Ellie has 16 vases of flowers. Each vase has 16 flowers. How many flowers does Ellie have in all?

266. A bookshelf can hold nine books. If there are five bookshelves in a room, how many books can the room hold in total?

267. Dominic can catch 14 fish per hour. How many fish can Dominic catch in seven hours?

268. Emily wants to make six flower arrangements, and each arrangement requires 13 flowers. How many flowers does Emily need in total?

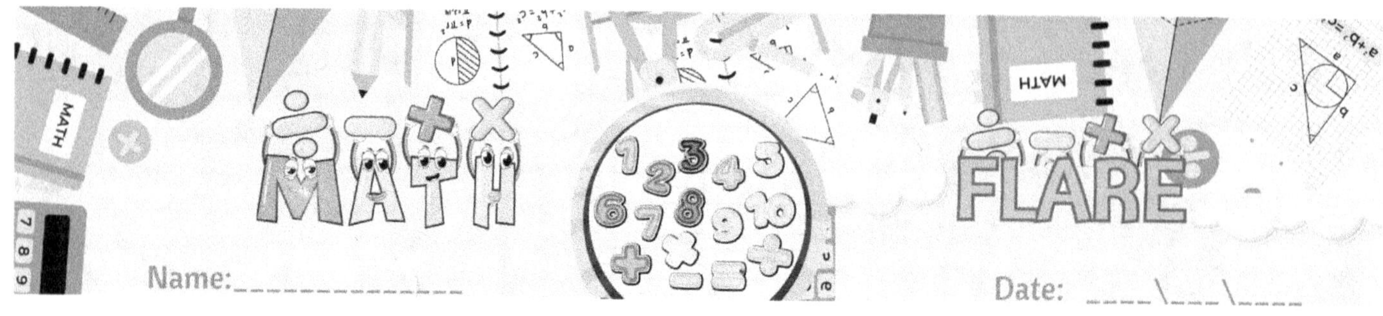

Division Word Problems

269. Kai is reading a book with 301 pages. If Kai wants to read the same number of pages every day, how many pages would Kai have to read each day to finish in seven days?

270. A rope is 1,479 meters long. If you cut it into 17 equal pieces, how long is each piece?

271. If Andrew has 84 trees and wants to share them equally among 14 friends, how many trees will each friend get?

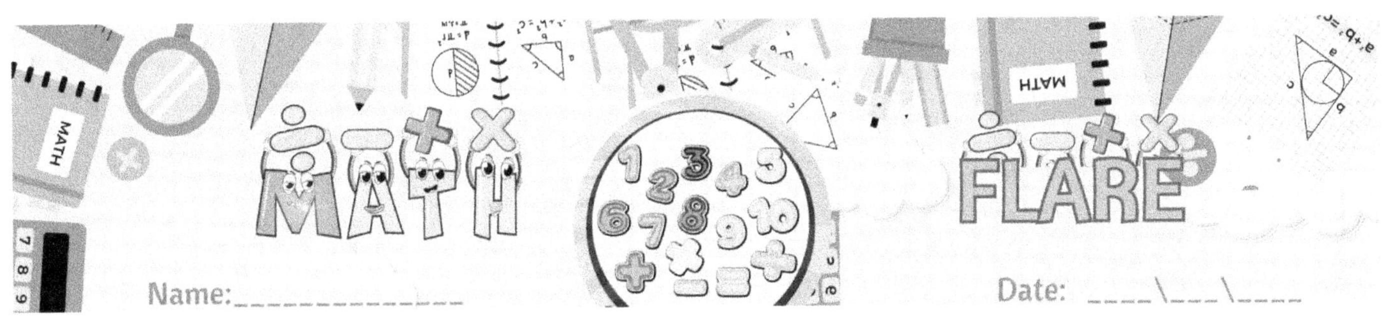

272. A car can travel 272 miles on 16 gallons of gas. How many miles can it travel on 1 gallon of gas?

273. Ella has 184 bags and wants to divide them equally among two people. How many bags will each person get?

274. A pool is 272 meters long. If it is divided into 16 equal parts, how long is each part?

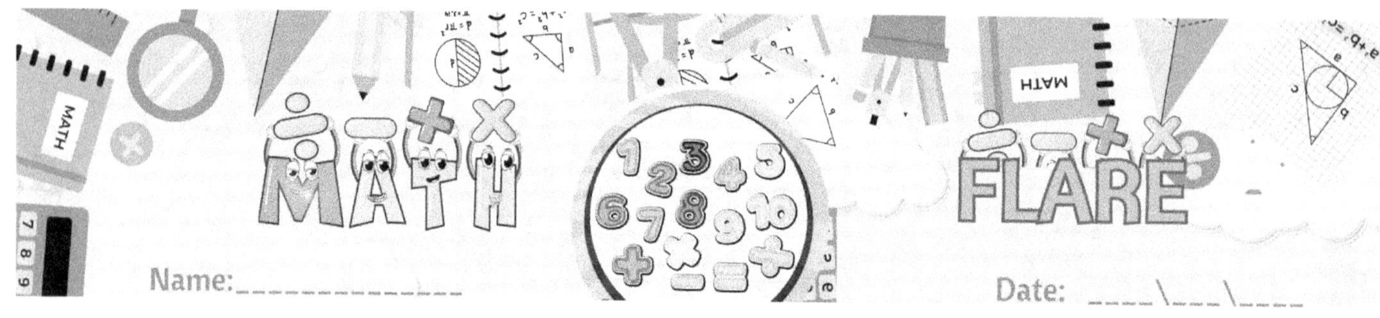

275. If a box contains 380 chocolates and each person can have 19 chocolates, how many people can be served from that box?

276. If a garden is 702 feet long and it is divided into nine equal parts, how long is each part?

277. A roll of tape is 494 feet long. If Lily needs to cut the tape into 13 pieces that are all the same length, how long will each piece be?

278. At a restaurant, 20 friends decided to divide the bill equally. If each person paid $six, then what was the total bill?

279. If Addison has 156 phones and wants to distribute them equally to 12 students, how many phones will each student get?

280. Aubree has 261 cookies and wants to divide them equally into three bags. How many cookies will be in each bag?

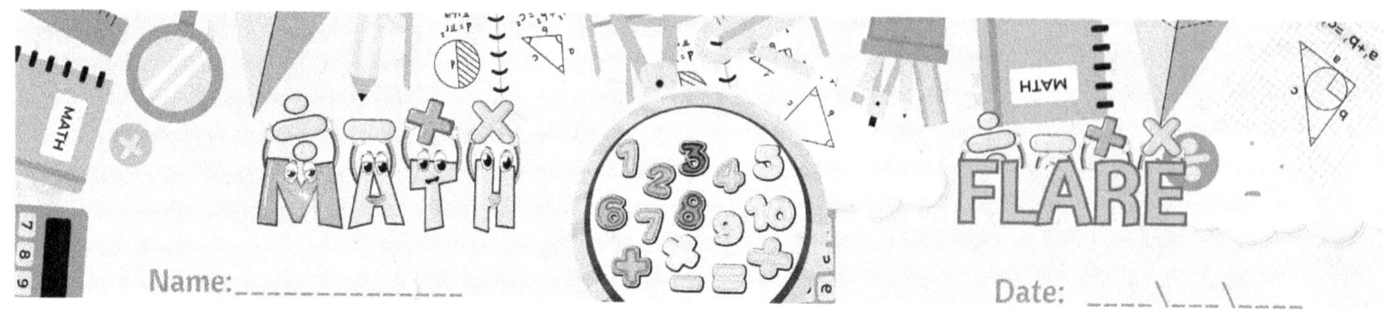

281. Isabella is packing 42 cupcakes into boxes. Each box can hold three cupcakes. How many boxes will Isabella need?

282. If a field is 68 acres and it is divided into two equal parts, how many acres is each part?

283. Evan has 424 pages of homework to do. If he wants to finish his homework in eight days, how many pages does he need to do each day?

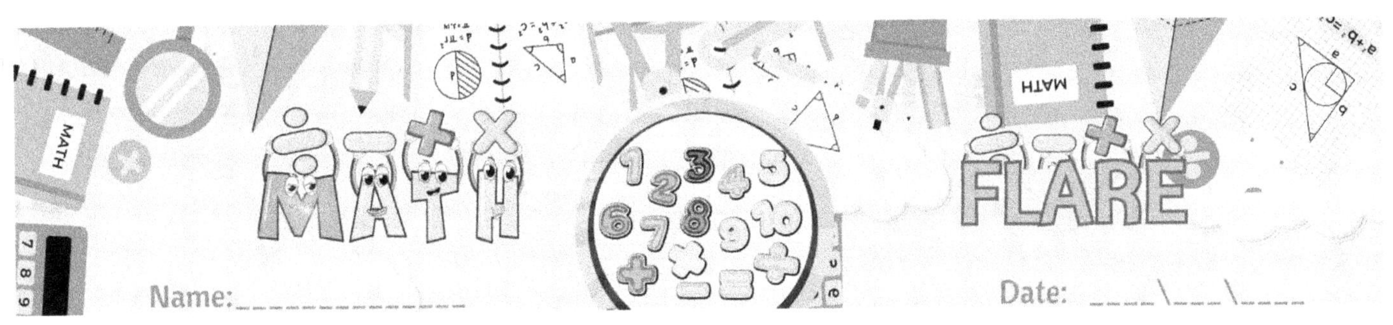

284. Luna is filling up water bottles. Each bottle holds 10 ounces of water. If Luna has 140 ounces of water, how many water bottles can she fill up?

285. Avery has $672 and she wants to buy 14 scrubs that cost the same amount. How much does each scrubs cost?

286. Camila baked 504 cakes for a party. If she wants to divide them into 12 equal portions, how many cakes will each portion have?

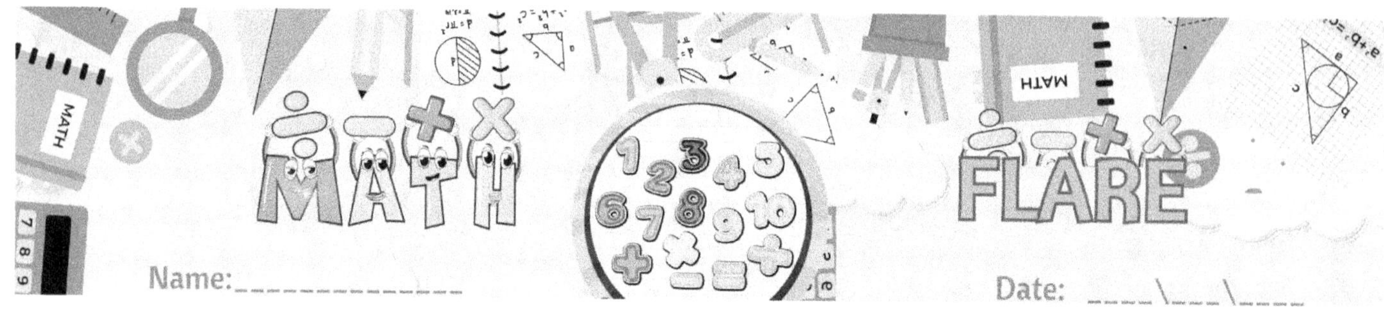

287. It takes Valentina 49 minutes to write 1 page. How many pages can Valentina write in 245 minutes?

288. Aurora made 186 cookies for a bake sale. She put the cookies in bags, with three cookies in each bag. How many bags did she have for the bake sale?

289. If the pizzas have 798 slices and is divided equally among 19 people, how many slices will each person get?

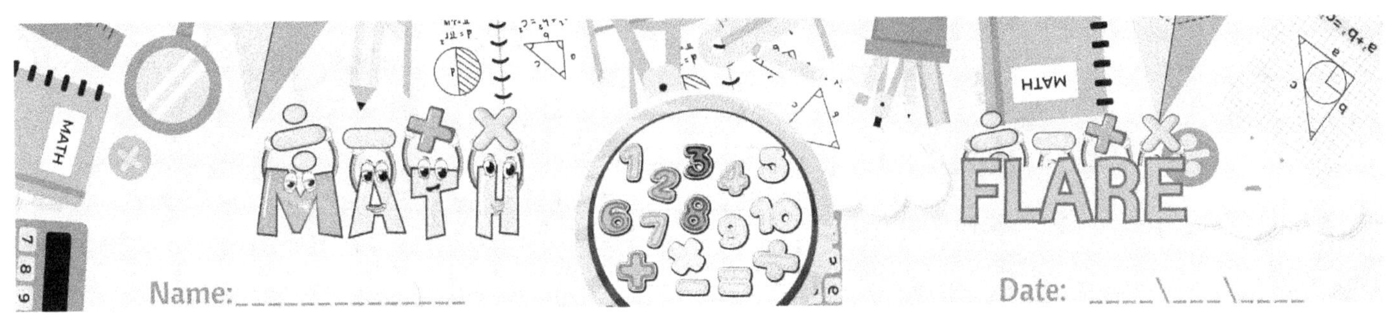

290. A box of balls has 1,260 balls. If 15 children each get an equal number of balls, how many balls will each child get?

291. How many 13 cm pieces of rope can you cut from a rope that is 481 cm long?

292. Samuel can type 104 words in 13 minutes. How many words can he type in 1 minute?

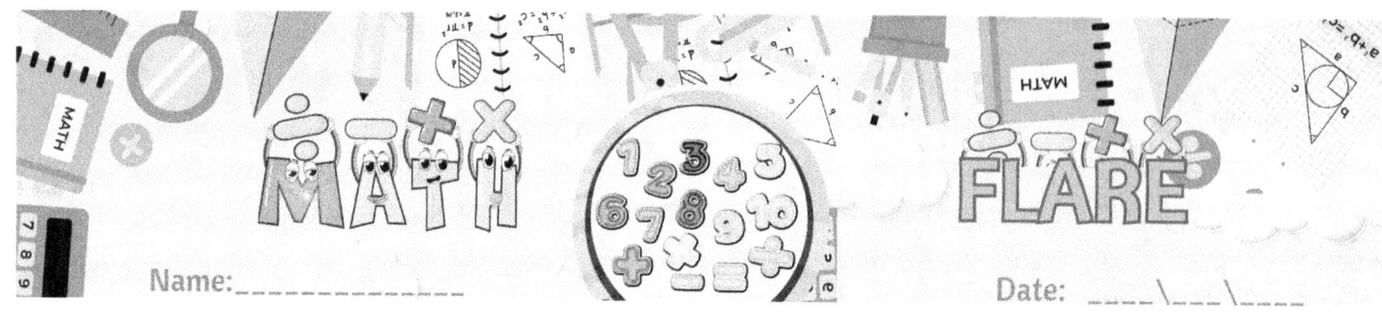

293. Peyton can run 117 miles in 13 hours. How many miles can she run in 1 hour?

294. If Brielle has 532 pens and wants to distribute them equally to 19 students, how many pens will each student get?

295. If Chloe has 249 clocks and wants to divide them equally among three friends, how many clocks will each friend get?

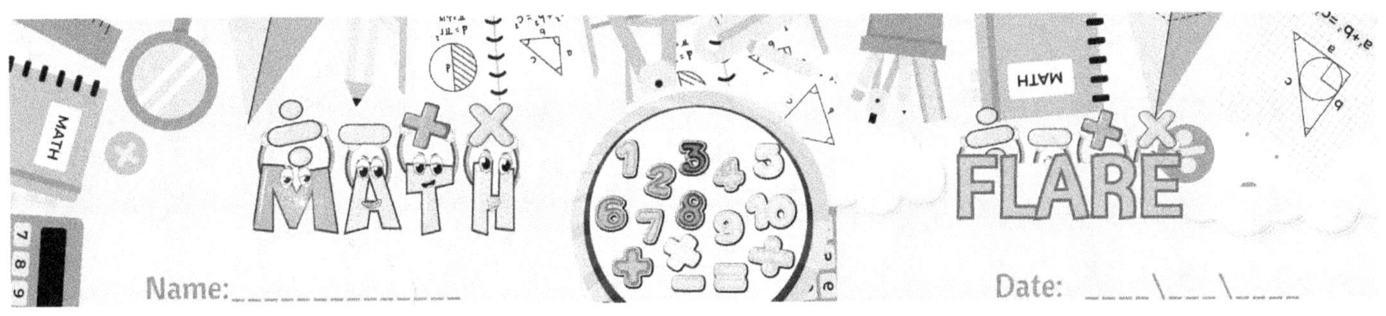

296. Scarlett bought six calculators for a total of $102. How much did each calculators cost?

297. If a store sells eight books for $752 how much will each books cost?

298. If a garden is 832 feet wide and it is divided into 16 equal parts, how wide is each part?

ANSWERS

Page 1:   Multi Digit Multiplication

1. 398,034,630
2. 128,154,666
3. 691,978,518
4. 392,198,092
5. 166,390,942
6. 57,143,580
7. 300,377,352
8. 481,289,552
9. 116,484,108
10. 101,993,120
11. 168,081,120
12. 81,694,446
13. 46,295,980
14. 193,222,880
15. 351,042,393
16. 179,025,080
17. 372,143,680
18. 358,209,324
19. 61,372,530
20. 153,116,970
21. 658,078,116
22. 200,633,664
23. 117,724,541
24. 421,772,956
25. 453,396,480
26. 204,344,256
27. 119,678,952
28. 281,632,020
29. 249,601,034
30. 102,142,029
31. 399,696,402
32. 163,885,716
33. 691,990,400
34. 658,167,786
35. 72,604,064
36. 346,797,944
37. 459,873,568
38. 224,622,900
39. 705,926,819
40. 78,185,640
41. 187,971,693
42. 76,472,192
43. 277,606,747
44. 265,916,025
45. 277,079,616
46. 184,172,814
47. 168,297,129
48. 381,141,432
49. 537,422,655
50. 241,116,360

Page 7:   Long Division

51. 142,358
52. 34,716
53. 14,500.5
54. 54,104.4

55. 19,431.1   56. 39,751.4   57. 35,745.6   58. 38,894.1

59. 17,607.2   60. 129,602.3   61. 82,491.7   62. 60,905.3

63. 201,276.5   64. 7,383.7   65. 60,697.9   66. 30,199

67. 86,715.7   68. 130,381.6   69. 24,155.9   70. 45,844.1

71. 38,105.1   72. 15,383.7   73. 43,743.1   74. 56,186.7

75. 70,449.1   76. 52,345.1   77. 48,038.8   78. 54,327.3

Page 14: Long Division: Remainders

79. 9,943 R17   80. 9,012 R13   81. 33,384 R12   82. 11,916 R8

83. 23,861 R2   84. 19,149 R36   85. 10,170 R17   86. 6,414 R27

87. 49,171 R5   88. 13,380 R6   89. 3,435 R36   90. 10,816 R0

91. 26,108 R5   92. 3,242 R43   93. 26,316 R28   94. 4,599 R0

95. 11,660 R34   96. 38,311 R14   97. 14,469 R33   98. 10,172 R19

99. 4,660 R3   100. 15,052 R4   101. 32,113 R8   102. 14,827 R42

103. 18,291 R27   104. 29,272 R5   105. 10,424 R9   106. 18,358 R21

107. 21,741 R30   108. 27,548 R22   109. 9,633 R21   110. 54,725 R4

111. 24,696 R16   112. 17,113 R26   113. 3,064 R0   114. 3,893 R19

115. 19,473 R26   116. 29,198 R3   117. 7,384 R15   118. 42,787 R1

119. 40,684 R8   120. 14,895 R12   121. 3,271 R27   122. 31,959 R7

123. 20,328 R18   124. 57,159 R8   125. 9,145 R1   126. 9,567 R21

127. 7,428 R6   128. 14,059 R8   129. 6,442 R13   130. 18,553 R25

131. 76,743 R2   132. 21,310 R9   133. 4,858 R18   134. 23,569 R26

135. 5,777 R20   136. 65,196 R5   137. 11,456 R22   138. 3,717 R24

139. 40,994 R2   140. 5,070 R42   141. 30,995 R2   142. 7,100 R0

143. 16,234 R34   144. 32,586 R5   145. 85,592 R5   146. 6,073 R20

147. 19,547 R8   148. 45,689 R2   149. 29,763 R0   150. 3,146 R38

151. 42,473 R4   152. 22,134 R19   153. 13,452 R8   154. 12,147 R14

155. 16,373 R6   156. 17,132 R12   157. 13,173 R1   158. 17,981 R38

159. 25,921 R23   160. 33,508 R17   161. 39,821 R8   162. 43,371 R11

163. 27,742 R17   164. 70,492 R3   165. 17,596 R4   166. 11,788 R15

167. 15,176 R11   168. 21,256 R11   169. 5,296 R20   170. 34,210 R14

171. 17,813 R8   172. 41,527 R17   173. 18,783 R3   174. 21,033 R18

175. 17,251 R36   176. 8,660 R19   177. 9,812 R13   178. 10,828 R5

Page 39: Using the Power of 10

179. 100,000   180. 20,000   181. 1,000,000   182. 2,000,000

183. 900.0   184. 4   185. 100,000   186. 5,000,000

187. 20.00   188. 10.00   189. 2,000,000   190. 900

191. 3.000   192. 70   193. 9,000,000   194. 10,000

195. 3.000   196. 100.0   197. 5   198. 900,000

199. 900,000   200. 700,000   201. 100   202. 3,000,000

203. 60,000   204. 200,000   205. 3   206. 20,000

207. 600.0   208. 40   209. 600   210. 500,000

211. 800.0   212. 400   213. 2   214. 3

215. 800,000   216. 20   217. 7,000,000   218. 20.00

219. 500,000   220. 90.00   221. 3   222. 10

223. 300.0   224. 10,000   225. 50,000   226. 200

227. 2   228. 200.0   229. 4.000   230. 700,000

231. 4   232. 900.0   233. 5,000,000   234. 400

235. 1,000,000   236. 8,000,000   237. 500.0   238. 800,000

Page 44:   Multiplication Word Problems

239. 380   240. 77   241. 32   242. 153   243. 95   244. 255

245. 98   246. 198   247. 70   248. 153   249. 340   250. 140

251. 112   252. 48   253. 182   254. 26   255. 169   256. 119

257. 144   258. 153   259. 340   260. 16   261. 60   262. 34

263. 400   264. 323   265. 256   266. 45   267. 98   268. 78

Page 54:   Division Word Problems

269. 43   270. 87   271. 6   272. 17   273. 92   274. 17   275. 20

276. 78   277. 38   278. 120   279. 13   280. 87   281. 14   282. 34

283. 53   284. 14   285. 48   286. 42   287. 5   288. 62   289. 42

290. 84   291. 37   292. 8   293. 9   294. 28   295. 83   296. 17

297. 94   298. 52